by Mike Maunder and Sigrid van der Zee
Maps by Rutger Jesse

On Foot
in North Lesvos

Contents

Authors' Note   IV

Preface   V

Introduction   VII

Walks around Molivos

  1   A Short Stroll through the Molivos Olive Groves 1

  2   Ancient Mithimna and Modern Molivos 3

  3   A Circuit through the Hills behind Molivos 10

  4   Through the Hills from Molivos to Petra 13

  5   Through the Valleys from Molivos to Vafios 16

  6   Molivos to Vafios through Keramotis 20

  7   Molivos to Petri 25

  8   Molivos to the Hot Springs of Eftalou and back..................29

  9   Hills, Valleys, and Sea 35

On Foot in North Lesvos

Authors' Note

Walk 19: Petri to Stipsi

A local farmer has blocked this route where it leaves the road at Petri with a high wire fence and locked gate.

We have tried, without success to get the gate unlocked, or to find an alternative route.

Therefore we regret that, as of late 2012, it is not possible to follow this walk.

Other routes may have changed slightly since this book was published. For the latest information please see the Stop Press page of our website, http://www.lesvoswalks.net/html/stop_press.html

Mike Maunder & Sigrid van der Zee

Walks around Petra and Anaxos

10 Petra to Petri or Vafios through the Ligonas Valley (Valley of the Mills) 39
11 Petra to Petri 46
12 Petra to Lafionas and return 49
13 Petra to Anaxos..53
14 Anaxos to Ambelia Beach..55
15 Lafionas to Anaxos 58
16 From Lafionas around Roudi to Agios Alexandros 62

Further Afield

17 From Vafios to Molivos or Petra 65
18 Vafios to Stipsi round the Mountain 69
19 Petri to Stipsi 73
20 A Forest Walk to Klapados and Lafionas.........................76
21 A Circular Walk from Skoutaros to Tsichrada 79
22 Eftalou to Skala Sikaminias 84
23 Skala Sikaminias to Sikaminia circular routes 88
24 Argenos, Chalikas and Vigla Circular 97
25 A Circular walk from Agia Paraskevi to Klopedi, Taxiarchis Monastery, and Kremasti Bridge 103

Authors' Note

All the routes in this book are described as they were when we last walked them, between October 2009 and March 2010.

While we have taken every care to ensure that our descriptions are complete and accurate, and that the routes we suggest can be completed safely and enjoyably, we can of course accept no responsibility for any difficulties you may encounter while using this book.

This is a living, working landscape, which is one of its many attractions. Change is constant, and quite rightly takes place primarily for the convenience of its residents rather than its visitors. So in all probability you will find some things which are not as they were when we were writing.

Between us we live eighteen months of each year on Lesvos, and much of that time is spent walking. Any significant changes that we find will be posted on our website, www.lesvoswalks.net, in downloadable and printable form. If, meanwhile, you find anything that you think should be noted, please send us an email at changes@lesvoswalks.net, or write to the address on the copyright page.

Preface to the 4th Edition

Much has changed in Lesvos since I wrote the first, much slimmer, version of this book in the winter of 1999. Purely from a walker's point of view, some of the changes have been detrimental - more land has been fenced and gates locked (and some fences have become more formidable), old footpaths have been bulldozed into tracks, or obliterated completely, and tracks have become asphalt roads, so losing much of their appeal as walking routes (while, of course, making life easier for residents)

At the same time, there have been many positive changes. There is a growing awareness both from holiday companies and local municipalities that many visitors wish to explore on foot. Encouraged with financial help from the island's tourist board and EC agencies, many municipalities have begun to clear, map and waymark old routes around places of interest. Several companies have begun to offer walking holidays in various parts of the island, and there are also multi-lingual guides leading day excursions on foot.

Another change. In 1999 I was a newly-retired sixty-year-old. Ten years later, inevitably, I am ten years older, still fit, but for how much longer? So when it became time for this new edition of 'On Foot in North Lesvos', and I was discussing this with my friend Sigrid van der Zee, I was delighted and encouraged when she immediately suggested that we should collaborate. Sigrid has lived on Lesvos for many years, working for much of the time as a guide, and knows many parts of the island much better than I do. For the past few years she has been responsible for translating the book's annual update leaflets into Dutch. As she also has the great advantage of being thirty years younger than me I'm looking forward to her taking the book forward when I have finally retired to my zimmer frame.

This new edition is therefore a joint effort: we have checked the routes together, removing some that were no longer viable or interesting, adding others, and hopefully eliminating some of the embarrassing mistakes that arose from me working alone. We have also taken the opportunity to bring the book into the 21st century by adding GPS co-ordinates at key points. We hope you will enjoy using it!

Mike Maunder

April 2010

Introduction

About the Fourth Edition

Until recently most visitors to Lesvos came to the island on one or two week package holidays and stayed in the northern villages of Molivos, Petra or Anaxos. (This is how we both arrived for the first time at different times in the past). For that reason previous editions of "On Foot in North Lesvos" concentrated almost exclusively on walks starting from one or other of those resorts, and exploring an area, loosely defined as North Lesvos, between the coast and the Lepetimnos mountain range behind it to the south. Routes were designed so that by following one or more the reader would be brought back to the starting point, thus avoiding the need for any form of transport other than his or her own feet.

For this edition we have broadly kept to this model: however an increasing number of returning visitors, independent travellers, and hire cars on the roads have encouraged us to go slightly further afield and add a selection of circular walks needing a car or taxi to reach the start/finish point.

Otherwise, while the majority of walks have been retained, at least in part, from previous editions, we have also added several new ones, the product of our exploration, separately and together, over the past years. We have also taken the opportunity to completely revise every existing route, using the many changes that have taken place on the ground over the last few years to add new sections to make routes more interesting or scenically attractive, and where possible removing stretches where what were once dirt roads or tracks have disappeared under asphalt or concrete.

The principle of the book remains the same – to help you to get to know this beautiful and fascinating island a little better, and to encourage your own exploration. To quote the final words of the previous introduction:-

"Above all, don't be afraid to explore. Many of the walks here are

the result of thinking 'I wonder where that goes', and going to find out. Many, indeed most, tracks and paths will turn out to be dead ends, but you will come across more views, more wildlife, and maybe some interesting people. And it is very difficult to get completely lost; there will almost always be a visible landmark, or the sea, to aim for. So:

Safe and Happy Walking!

"He who drinks the water, forgets it not and returns'"

How to use the book

Please read the following notes before setting off – this should help you get the most out of your walks.

Preparation, Equipment, etc

With a few exceptions, the walks in this book are walks, not 'treks'; most of them easy, or, at most, of medium difficulty. Any exceptions are noted in the introductions to each walk.

They are mainly along well-defined tracks or footpaths, and call for no special clothing or equipment. Long trousers are advisable to protect your legs against the Greek vegetation, which is almost invariably spiny and aggressive, especially once it has dried out during the summer. For your feet, good trainers with solid non-slip soles are quite sufficient. That you take a hat, sun protection and plenty of water should go without saying. A mobile phone can be useful in case of emergency, though you should be aware that signal coverage can be very patchy (and in some places will come via Turkey, making a local phone call for a taxi very expensive!)

Please read through the descriptions of each walk before setting out and judge its length and difficulty against your party's capabilities. The best months for walking are May, early June, September and October; in midsummer, July and August, it can get very hot and shade will be in short supply. Allow time for a slower pace and more rests, take even more water and be aware of the danger of overheating and dehydration. Also the vegetation will be tinder-dry; be especially careful not to start any fires.

We have tried to make the descriptions in this book detailed enough to make maps and other aids superfluous, though we have added GPS co-ordinates at key points for readers who wish to use them.

Co-ordinates, Distances and Times

At each significant point you will find bracketed information in the text similar to this:- *[2. 22.74'/11.08', 1.69km/190m, 5 mins]*

Reference

[2. 22.74'/11.08', 1.69km/190m, 5 mins] This cross-references to the map accompanying each walk.

GPS Co-ordinates

*[2. **22.74'/11.08'**, 1.69km/190m, 5 mins]* These are shown as minutes of latitude (N) and longitude (E) to the nearest 1/100th of a minute. They were established on the ground using a handheld Garmin e-Trex receiver, and subsequently double-checked where possible against Google Earth readings (the Google Earth images of the area are not always of high enough definition to do this accurately).

All the walks fall within 39°N and 26°E, which we have therefore omitted to save space, except for the first reference in each walk. At this latitude 1/100th of a minute is approximately 15 metres.

Distances

*[22.74'/11.08', **1.69km/190m**, 5 mins]* These are also taken from e-Trex readings, and are the calculated distances from the starting point of the walk, and from the previous reading.

The approximate total distance for each walk is shown at the beginning of the description.

Timings

*[22.74'/11.08', 1.69km/190m, **5 mins**]* These are the actual elapsed times, at a reasonably brisk walking pace, from the previous point. They are watch times, and include brief halts to check landmarks, tie shoe-laces, sip water etc, but not longer rest breaks.

It is advisable to try one or two of the shorter walks first, to measure your speed against ours, and make the necessary adjustments before tackling the longer routes.

The approximate total time for each walk is shown at the beginning of the description.

Definitions

We have tried to be consistent in our use of words, though in some cases, particularly with 'dirt roads' and 'tracks' the distinctions might become blurred, and even change depending on the time of year, weather conditions etc when we wrote the description.

Broadly, therefore:-

Dirt Roads are unsurfaced, but compacted and (usually) graded. They are used by all vehicles apart from buses, though taxi drivers are also often reluctant. They are often sign-posted with green finger-posts hand-lettered in white.

Tracks are also wide enough to take vehicles, but are often privately bull-dozed to give access to a particular piece of land or building, left un-compacted, and deteriorate rapidly if unused.

Paths (Monopatia – μονοπάτια and Kalderimia – καλντερίμια) are footpaths, either formal, often walled on either side and running between fields or olive groves, or informal paths across open land or olive groves. The former are often kalderimia, the old cobbled paths between settlements, now in many cases fallen into disrepair.

Gates: Almost all land in this part of Lesvos is fenced or walled. Most gates are to keep stock in or mark property boundaries rather than keep people out, and may be used unless padlocked or firmly wired shut. They can be anything from a strand of barbed wire to a wrought-iron creation set between stone pillars; most popular are lengths of concrete reinforcing mesh and old single bed frames (which are just the right size for a gate across a track). You will also find barriers of brushwood piled across gaps to prevent animals from straying. As you would anywhere, always leave them as you find them. While we have noted gates and other barriers which we know to be reasonably permanent, they do frequently come and go, and you may well find ones which we have not.

Farm buildings can range from large modern concrete cattle-sheds through ancient stone byres to sheds pieced together from scrap timber and sheet metal.

River- and stream-beds are usually dry, or carrying only a trickle of water, during the holiday season from May to October. In the wet season, from late October on, or after unseasonable storms, however, they can become torrents or subject to flash floods. While these dates used to be predictable (there were always thunderstorms in the second week of October), climate change seems to be bringing more storms at other times of the year: if you are planning a walk that involves crossing, or walking along, a stream- or river-bed, take extra care in unfavourable weather.

Flora and Fauna

This is not intended to be a wildlife guide, and we have not attempted to identify the plants and animals that you may meet, beyond the obvious trees; oaks, pines, and the ubiquitous olives used as landmarks. Efstathiadis of Athens publishes well-illustrated field guides to wild flowers, trees, birds, etc. in several languages, which are available in local bookshops. There is also 'Wild Flowers of Greece' a comprehensive and beautifully illustrated guide published by Mediterraneo Editions of Crete.

As mentioned previously, Greek vegetation, almost by definition, is aggressive. It has spikes, spines and thorns and will use them on any unprotected flesh, especially at ankle level. Particularly in summer, anything described here as 'pasture' or 'meadow' will consist almost entirely of thorn bushes and thistles. And if those don't get you the holly oak will!

Most wild animals will sense you before you see them, and get out of your way. You may see red squirrels and foxes, and if you are very lucky a pine marten. There are tortoises, terrapins and frogs in ponds and cisterns, and of course lizards of various sizes and colours everywhere.

There is one poisonous snake in Lesvos, the Nose-horned Viper, whose bite is extremely dangerous and often fatal, but it is described as "slow and rather phlegmatic, not very irascible" and you are unlikely to come across a live one except possibly as a rustling in the undergrowth as you pass. You are much more likely to see the plain brown Montpellier Snake (easily confused with the legless Glass Lizard), or the slim European Cat Snake. Both of these are technically venomous, but as their fangs are at the back of the jaw you are unlikely to be bitten unless you try to stick a finger down their throat!

Lesvos is a paradise for bird-watchers, as it is on spring and autumn migration routes, but if you are a bird-watcher you will know this already and have come prepared.

Dogs, of course, are everywhere. Like their owners, the vast majority of island dogs are friendly: the frantic barking of a tethered dog more often comes from boredom and a wish for attention than from aggressiveness. However it is of course sensible to use normal caution when dealing with them. Occasionally farmers use groups of dogs to guard their flocks, and these can become intimidating. Where we have come across these regularly we mention it in the text.

It is also worth noting that the majority of dogs you may come across will be working animals, not pets, and are not cosseted as domestic dogs might be in northern Europe. Their owners have hard lives, often for little reward, and so may their dogs. However most are well looked after and there is very little deliberate cruelty.

Useful Information

Local Transport

Buses

During the holiday season a shuttle bus service runs along the coast between Eftalou and Anaxos.

The main service bus from Molivos to Mitilini via Petra and Kalloni runs anything from one to six times a day depending on the season, day of the week, school and public holidays etc. The tourist information office next door to the National Bank of Greece in Molivos usually has the current timetable posted in the window, and can advise on changes. Buses to villages off the main road, even quite large places such as Stipsi, tend to be infrequent, and organised as feeder services connecting at Kalloni.

Taxis

As everywhere in Greece, taxis are plentiful, convenient, and relatively cheap. There are taxi stands at Molivos (phone 22530 71480) and Petra (22530 42022 or 22530 41169).

Stipsi, Pelopi, and Ypsilometopo all have their own taxis.

Emergency Phone Numbers

Police, Ambulance etc: 112

Fire: 199

What's in a Name - Mithimna or Molivos?

The original name of the city-state which ruled this area of Lesvos was Mithimna or Methimna (Μήθυμνα). Thought to have been founded in the 14th century BC, it was second only to Mitilini among the six states which divided the island. (The others were Eressos, Antissa - on the coast north-east of the modern town - Pyrra, on the Gulf of Kalloni, and Arisvi, today a suburb of Kalloni on the main road to Mitilini, but originally on a hill rising out of the plain just to the north). According to the ancient Greek writer Parthenios, and local legend, Achilles sacked Mithimna during the Trojan War (probably c1200BC)

During the Byzantine period it became known as Molivos (Μόλυβος), which it remained throughout the Turkish occupation from 1462 until 1912. Since then the official name of the town has reverted to Mithimna, but we have adopted the popular name throughout this book.

Starting Points

Unless otherwise mentioned, all walks from Molivos start at the junction by the pine wood and farmers' co-operative, near the sports field.

Those from Petra start from the sea-front square outside the 'Kantina' bar and Womens' Co-operative guest-house.

A Short Stroll through the Molivos Olive Groves

Total distance 2.25 kilometres

 Walking time 40 mins

After a day on the beach this short, level, forty-minute stroll is just the thing to prepare for that pre-dinner drink or three. It also makes a gentle introduction to the longer and more strenuous walks ahead.

From the start *[1. 39°21.97'/26°10.86']*, take the concrete road running down to the right of the pine wood and bear left with the Liokambi apartment complex on your left.

Immediately after this the track divides by a small cottage on the left, with a path leading off to the right. *[2. 21.81'/10.93', 365m, 5 mins]* Ignore this and continue on the walled track ahead, passing a house on the right. The track finally bends to the left and ends. *[3. 21.74'/11.05', 590m/225m, 5 mins]*

Continue on the path to the right past gates into olive groves and a house behind high wrought iron gates on the right. Shortly after passing a white stone archway under a tiled roof on the left (which leads into another olive grove) turn right at a T-junction on to a crossing track. *[4. 21.67'/11.13', 780m/190m, 4 mins]* (For a shorter version of this walk turn left here).

After about 20 metres the track bends left to pass a house on the right and continues to a river. *[5. 21.57'/11.28', 1.09km/310m, 5 mins]* (This is the river which passes under the Molivos-Petra road at the twin bridges near the Vafios road junction and emerges into the sea halfway along the beach).

Follow the track as it swings left along the river bank with a cottage and garden wall on the left and turn left again at the next junction. Continue with vegetable gardens on the right, and go left where the track next divides. *[6. 21.70'/11.29', 1.35km/260m, 5 mins]*

Go over a slight rise and then right at the next junction leaving a rock face on your left. *[7. 21.71'/11.18', 1.52km/170m, 3 mins]* (The short cut rejoins here from the left).

After another five minutes the pine wood will appear on the left and the sports ground on the right as the track brings you back to your starting point. *[8. 21.97'/10.86, 2.20km/680m, 10 mins]*

Ancient Mithimna and Modern Molivos

2

Total distance 4.25 kilometres

 Walking time 1 hour 30 mins

but allow a full morning to visit the castle, browse, stop and stare, sit in tavernas etc.

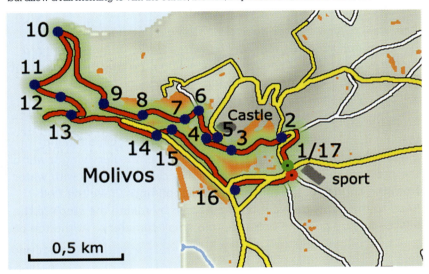

The Molivos area has been continuously settled since the Bronze Age, first in the valley running down to the sea to the east of the town, now occupied by the Aphrodite Hotel. From about the middle of the thirteenth century BC the city grew on its present site, plus the plateau of the Dapia, behind the harbour, in all about double the area of the modern town.

Looked at from below, the main street of Molivos (ΟΔΟΣ 17 ΝΟΕΜΒΡΙΟΥ - 17 November or ΑΓΟΡΑ - Market) runs across the cliff like a giant bow, with the harbour road as the bowstring. From the highest point of the bow its arrow, ΟΔΟΣ ΚΑΣΤΡΟΥ (Castle Street), continues upwards towards the castle. Above and to the right of these streets a maze of cobbled lanes, terraces and staircases rises steeply up to the castle, filled with houses large and small, old and new. Strict controls ensure that new buildings in the town conform to traditional styles, and rapidly blend in with their surroundings: for instance the OTE telephone exchange on the harbour road and the medical centre in the Agora were built in 1999. The best way to discover this part of town is to spend a morning getting lost in it, remembering that heading downhill will always (eventually) bring you back to the main street or the school.

This walk explores other quarters of the old and new town, with plenty of opportunities for relaxing with a drink, or being tempted by the wide variety of specialist shops along the way. Time it so that you arrive at the castle during opening hours - normally 0800 - 1900 daily (except Mondays) during the summer season.

From the start *[1. 39°21.97'/26°10.86']*, take the road opposite leading uphill, signposted to the castle (Κάστρο). On a mound diagonally across to the right you will see the one surviving tower of the pre-Roman aqueduct that supplied ancient Mithimna with water from the springs of the mountains of Lepetimnos. Take the first bend to the right, then cut off the hairpin by taking the steps to the left leading up past the entrance to a small cemetery. At the top of

the steps turn left back on to the road, then immediately, when the road swings right, continue ahead. *[2. 22.08'/10.83', 270m, 5 mins]*

This road quickly ends, leading into a paved, stepped street, which bears right with railings on the left. Where they end bear left. One of the three main churches of Molivos, Αγ Κυριακή, lies just ahead. To visit the church, go through the gate, and walk through the courtyard, exiting through the gate at the far end. Otherwise keep to the street which leads along to the right of the church wall, and continue to the second church gate, ignoring streets up to the right.

Ignore the steps down to the left, then at the next junction keep right, and then immediately left uphill. *[10 mins]* Ignore the first paths going off to left and right, and then at the next fork keep right. *[3. 22.05'/10.65']* At the next fork keep right again, with railings on your left, and immediately right once again, leading up to the church gate of Αγ Ταξιαρχων (Church of the Archangels). *[4. 22.08'/10.56', 5 mins]* Then go to the right up the steps, and at the top turn right to the Castle entrance. *[5. 22.08'/10.61', 760m/490m, 5 mins]*

The castle as it survives today is mainly Byzantine, built on the site of much more ancient fortifications dating from the 9th or 10th century BC. It was repaired and extended in 1373AD by Francisco Gattelusi, the Genoese ruler of Lesvos of the time, and later by the Ottoman occupiers of the island, and these days is used for occasional concerts and theatrical performances. Note the Turkish inscription that survives over the entrance gate. The panoramic views from the castle walls towards the interior of the island and across the strait to the Turkish coast, (though not recommended to any sufferer from vertigo), are in themselves worth the admission charge.

On leaving the castle turn right along the path past the Panorama taverna and follow the street running downhill. Take the second turning to the left opposite the sign pointing back to ΚΑΣΤΡΟ *[6. 22.16'/10.55', 4 mins]* and continue down the stepped street to a crossing with a bakery on the left. *[7. 22.14'/10.49', 4 mins]*

The main shopping street lies ahead under a canopy of vines awaiting our return but for now we turn right. Although there is currently no street sign, this is ΟΔΟΣ ΑΡΓΥΡΗ ΕΦΤΑΛΙΩΤΗ (Argiris Eftaliotis, the modern Greek poet, whose bust is in the forecourt of the municipal art gallery, and whose town house, with a plaque beside the gate, we pass on our left a few metres down this street)

Continue down through ΠΛΑΤΕΙΑ ΑΝΔΡΕΑ ΚΥΡΙΑΚΟΥ (Andrea Kyriakos Square) where two massive trees give shade to the open air Tropicana Taverna and the two impressive nineteenth century mansions in their walled gardens to the right, and take the second right turn. *[8. 22.19'/10.34', 5mins]* Above on the right you will see the police station and local tax office housed in the old Ottoman administration buildings situated on top of the ancient city walls. Just after the last house on the right there is a small entrance into the excavations of what appears to have been a Roman bath house.

A few metres further on turn right up steps through a gate in the wall into a field. *[9. 22.17'/10.21', 1.50km/740m, 6mins]* Follow the path across to meet a paved road leading down to the main town cemetery. Do not follow this, but turn sharp left on to the track that leaves the road at this point.

You are now in the Dapia, the site of the ancient city of Mithimna, which stretched from the castle to Cape Molivos, which lies behind the belt of trees ahead to the right. In 1895 a British archaeologist, W H D Rouse, noted that "Between the fortress and the sea is a wide stretch of land, the site of the old town, covered with thousands of potsherds and pieces of earthen ware", and this remains true today. Over the centuries the area has been

continuously cultivated and the remains scattered, but some sites are identifiable and have been partially excavated. Most recently, the construction of a new main sewer taking Molivos's waste water to a state of the art sewage works hidden in the valley ahead, has further disturbed the area, while revealing new archaeological sites.

The track leads downhill towards a car park and the ruins of an old windmill, but ends at a fence. Swing right a few metres earlier and join another track running parallel with the coastline. (We will pass the mill on our return!) When this track bends right *[10mins]* go left and walk across rough ground to Cape Molivos.
[10. 22.39'/10.05', 2.10km/600m, 5mins (seaward end)]

Leaving the cape, with your back to the sea, you will see a path along the clifftop to the right, leading through a gate into woodland. Follow this, and when the wood ends stay on it along the cliff edge as far as the next headland, where the cliff turns sharp left.
[11. 22.24'/09.96', 2.50km/400m, 10mins]

From here head diagonally inland with the castle directly ahead. Pass worked masonry from the ancient city wall, and come to the ruins of ancient buildings with a section of paved courtyard and a well. Then cross to the small gate in the line of trees ahead, which brings you into the harbour car park, with the old windmill on your left. *[12. 22.21'/10.06', 2.70km/200m, 5 mins]* (At some seasons traces of an old circular threshing floor can also be seen in the field diagonally to the left).

Walk straight ahead out of the car park and turn right on to the road. Follow it down, round to the left, and then turn sharp right at the junction to reach the harbour.
[13. 22.15'/10.09', 2.90km/200m, 5 mins]

Take a while to explore the harbour (there is a water fountain in the wall beyond The Captain's Table taverna, one of the few remaining with its original Turkish inscription, and a small boatyard at the end of the quay where the local fishing caïques are repaired and built) and its galleries and tavernas. Then follow round the outer harbour - the quay here is where the larger fishing boats unload their catch

every evening - past the harbour church, Ag. Nikolaos, and back up the harbour road as it climbs along the cliff, with views to Vafios and along the beach to the Olive Press and beyond.

In the rear wall of the courtyard to the left of the OTE telephone exchange is a section of Lesvian polygonal masonry from the Archaic period (c500BC), with more lining the underground chamber in front. If the courtyard is closed this is visible from the lane behind, accessible from the steps to the right of the 'Pirates' bar, next to another fountain, this time with inscriptions in both Turkish and Greek, commemorating the donor as ΧΑΤΣΙΑΧΜΕΤΟΓΛΟΥ ΧΑΤΣΙΜΟΥΣΤΑΦΑ (Hatsiachmetoglu Hatsimustapha) in 1884.

Where the paved harbour road becomes tarmac and begins to run downhill take the cobbled fork left uphill *[14. 22.10'/10.39', 3.40km/500m, 10 mins]*, and in 50 metres fork left again, leaving the municipal art gallery (ΔΗΜΟΤΙΚΗ ΠΙΝΑΚΟΘΗΚΗ) and the bust of ΑΡΓΥΡΗ ΕΦΤΑΛΙΩΤΗ (Argiris Eftaliotis) on your right. As you near the top of this street there is a small junction on the right. Take the upper path through the entrance under the campanile, into the courtyard of the church of Ag. Pantelimon (Αγ Παντέλεημων). *[15. 22.09'/10.46', 3.50km/100m, 5 mins].* Here there are wonderful views from the harbour along the coast to the far west of the island. Exit through the gate at the far end of the courtyard and turn right into ΟΔΟΣ ΚΑΣΤΡΟΥ (Castle Street, aka The Agora).

A few metres down the hill on the left, above and behind the shops lining the street, are the decaying remains of the Ottoman public baths. A marble-tiled foyer led into an antechamber under a pierced domed roof, and thence into an impressive circular bathhouse, the walls lined with individual cubicles in white marble and with a marble floor, all under a large pierced dome. Unfortunately, the building is currently closed and in a state of collapse. There have long been plans, and sometimes funds, for its restoration, but at the time of writing it is only possible to snatch glimpses of the outside of the building from the open site opposite the Post Office.

Continue downhill to the square; ahead is the community hall bridging over the street. This was once the Ottoman mosque, with a well and basins in the forecourt for the faithful to wash before prayers, and the remains of its minaret on the wall above.

Walk on down ΟΔΟΣ 17 ΝΟΕΜΒΡΙΟΥ (Agora) under the hall to its junction with the harbour road. Twenty metres before the bottom of the hill another fountain on the left carries a Turkish inscription dated in Arabic numerals 1296 (1879AD).

Turn left past the excavated site of part of an ancient cemetery, and left again, with the school on your right and earlier cemetery excavations on your left, (there is more polygonal masonry visible here, dating these tombs also to the Archaic period).
[16. 21.94'/10.64', 3.90km/400m, 10 mins] Opposite the cemetery, the car park behind the school lies on the site of Mithimna's ancient theatre: with imagination it is possible to visualise the curved tiers of stone seats rising up the bank behind the parked cars. Finally continue up the hill to return to the starting point of your walk.
[17. 21.97'/10.86', 4.30km/400m, 10 mins]

A Circuit through the Hills behind Molivos

3

Total distance 6 kilometres

 Walking time 1 hour 30 mins

The paths and tracks criss-crossing through the hills behind Molivos give a number of opportunities for shortish circular walks.

Here is one suggestion:

From the start *[1. 39°21.97'/26°10.86'],* take the track to the left of the pine wood. Where the track divides at a rock face turn left over the rise. *[2. 21.71'/11.18', 720m, 8 mins]* After another two minutes there is a junction: carry straight on and follow the track as it bears round to the left.

At the next junction take the track to the right. *[3. 21.75'/11.33', 1.06km/340m, 5 mins]* (Continuing straight ahead at this point will bring you back in 10 minutes to the Molivos-Eftalou road, on the way passing the donkey farm belonging to Michaelis, leader of the donkey trekking excursions that start here).

After passing the race track belonging to the Pegasus Equestrian

Club of Mithimna (ΙΠΠΙΚΟΣ ΟΜΙΛΟΣ ΜΗΘΥΜΝΑΣ Ο ΠΗΓΑΣΟΣ) continue along the track with the river gorge on the right to a group of farm buildings on the right, and then wind uphill, ignoring tempting tracks on the right and left, over a small ridge, and, ignoring another track joining from the left (this merely leads back to the farm buildings on top of the mound to the left, and stops), come to a T-junction with the track from Molivos to the Argenos-Vafios road. *[4. 21.84'/12.43', 3.00km/1.94km, 35 mins]*

Turn left here to return to Molivos, following the main track as it leads down leaving the boundary of the Molivos-Sikaminia nature reserve to the right. In particular ignore the two tracks to the left; these lead to the Molivos municipal tip, hence, unfortunately, the rubbish scattered along this section of the walk. The track in this area has been straightened in places at various times, leaving several sections of the previous route leading nowhere - to avoid dead ends and, more seriously, precipices, stay on the main track leading downhill.

The track finally passes the Camping Mithimna campsite on the left and joins the Molivos-Eftalou road.
[5.22.17'/11.59', 4.40km/1.40km, 25 mins]

Turn left, and if you wish follow the main road for ten minutes back to the start of the walk.

Otherwise, after about fifty metres, where the main road swings left, take the road straight ahead on the right with the castle ahead in the distance. Follow this road, and take the second turning to the left on to a smooth dirt road. *[6. 22.25'/11.27', 4.90km/500m, 5 mins]* The road leads to a large modern house on the left, and then deteriorates into a track. Keep left at the next junction, by a well, and follow the path until it ends at a sloping rock-face. Bear right up across the rock for about fifty metres and then left to rejoin the path which leads between a fenced field on the left and a steep bank on the right up to the Molivos Castle road at the bend by the cemetery. *[7. 22.09'/10.89', 5.60km/700m, 10 mins]* To return to your starting point turn left and walk down the road.
[8. 21.97'/10.86', 5.86km/260m, 5 mins]

Through the Hills from Molivos to Petra

4

Total distance 6.5 kilometres

 Walking time 2 hours 15 mins

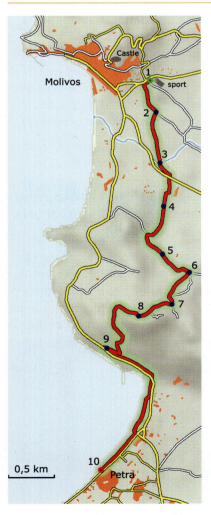

Everyone on holiday in Molivos visits Petra at least once, to visit the church on the rock from which the village takes its name, the Panagia Glykophiloussa (Παναγίας της Γλυκοφιλούσας - Our Lady of the Sweet Kiss), the c18 Macedonian-style Valeltzidaina mansion, and, of course, the long sandy beach. After recent road-building, this walk is now the only viable mainly off-road alternative to the coast road pavement.

From the start in Molivos *[1. 39°21.97'/26°10.86']*, take the concrete road to the right of the pine wood, follow it down past the Liokambi apartments *[2. 21.80'/10.93', 375m, 5 mins]*, and take the next right on to a walled path opposite a cottage. This leads between olive groves and orchards until after about ten minutes it arrives at a river bank.

Cross the river bed, climb the opposite bank on to a track, and bear left up past a small garden

13

centre on the left. *[3. 21.47'/10.98', 1.05km/675m, 10 mins]*

Continue over the crest ahead to meet the Molivos - Vafios road. Cross the road and follow the track opposite towards a group of modern houses, leaving a group of holiday apartments to the left. The track bends right and left past the first two houses and continues to a gate. *[4. 21.23'/10.98', 1.55km/500m, 10 mins]*

Go through and continue along the well-defined path through fields and scrubland, with a line of oak trees on the left. The path bears left with farm buildings visible to the right, and continues through rougher ground and denser scrub to another gate *[5. 20.97'/10.99', 2.05km/500m, 10 mins]* The rear entrance to an enclosed estate is visible on the left just ahead. (This is Karuna, a private centre used for spiritual retreats. The owners and guests value their privacy and isolation - **please respect it by keeping out of the property)**.

Beyond the gate leave the boundary of the estate to your left and follow a wandering path round as far as its main entrance. Turn right on the track leading away from the gates and then immediately right again through a gate on to a rough track running uphill. *[6. 20.85'/11.18', 2.50km/450m, 10 mins]* (The main track leads down to the Molivos - Petra road near the reservoir).

Continue up the hill. Ignore tracks to right and left, which lead to farm buildings. The uphill track bends left and continues to climb under woodland. Pass through a gate and after a few yards turn right. *[7. 20.66'/11.05', 3.02km/520m, 15 mins]* (This gate seems to come and go: if you don't find it make sure to turn right at the

first junction along this stretch)

Continue along this track, climbing gently through trees along the seaward side of the ridge. (There are several tempting tracks leading off uphill to the left - they are all dead ends leading to the top of the ridge and no further, but provide stunning views over the bay of Petra and the hills behind).

Eventually, after ten minutes, follow the track as it forks right and goes steeply downhill. *[8. 20.60'/10.80', 3.44km/420m, 10 mins]* (There is sometimes a flock of sheep, guarded by a gang of very noisy dogs, penned on this part of the hillside. The dogs egg each other on to get as close as possible to the heels of passing walkers. we have not known any of them to bite, but they can be intimidating if you are at all nervous). The track zigzags down - many of the steeper sections have been surfaced in concrete - to join the main Molivos - Petra coast road at an acute angle above Petra harbour (Ignore a well-defined track leading off to the left at the final right-hand bend). *[9. 20.42'/10.54', 4.55km/1.10km, 20 mins]*

Turn left on to the road and follow it down until it swings right at the bottom of the hill. Join the beach (or stay on the footpath) and walk along to Petra's main square with its tavernas and shops. *[10. 19.67'/10.51', 6.40km/1.85km, 25 mins]*

The taxi rank is also here for anyone wanting a ride home. The bus stop is about 200 metres back along the road towards Molivos, outside the public car-park.

Through the Valleys from Molivos to Vafios

Total distance 7.5 kilometres

Walking time 2 hours

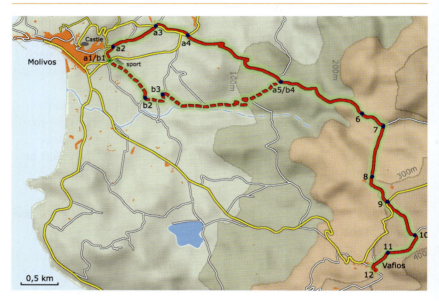

This walk leads through the valleys running south-east from Molivos up towards the Lepetimnos mountains, alongside the Molivos - Sikaminia nature reserve. This route is the one followed by the donkey-trekking expeditions to Vafios, so do not be surprised to be passed by (or overtake) a string of donkeys ridden by anxious holidaymakers under the supervision of Kostas or Michaelis.

There are two alternative starts to this walk. The first has the disadvantage that it leads past the Molivos municipal refuse tip. The approaches are covered with litter and dumped rubbish, but try to ignore these in favour of the sea views over Eftalou.

Start a. From the starting point *[a1. 39°21.97'/26°10.86']* take the road uphill towards the castle. It bends right (there are steps ahead) to lead round a small cemetery and then left again. Leave the road at the apex of the left-hand bend *[a2. 22.10'/10.89', 270m, 5 mins]*, and go down a footpath with a bank on the left and a field on the right. The path soon opens out on to a sloping rock face; go diagonally down to the right and pick the path up again at the bottom right-hand corner. Follow it along, keeping right where it forks by a small wellhead, and continue until you reach an asphalt road. *[a3. 22.25'/11.27' 930m/660m, 10 mins]*

Go right and follow the road (ignoring side-roads to tavernas etc) to join the Molivos - Eftalou road, and follow it for about fifty yards until it swings left. *[a4. 22.17'/11.59', 1.43km/500m, 5 mins]*

(If you wish, you can skip this first section by following the Eftalou road from the start to this junction).

Carry straight on up a side road, past a sign on the left marking the nature reserve, and the 'Camping Mithymna' site on the right. Continue past the 'No Entry' sign as the road becomes a track. Note the ΑΠΑΓΟΠΕΥΕΤΑΙ ΤΟ ΚΥΝΗΓΙ (Hunting Forbidden) signs on the left, which will be repeated at intervals along the length of the track as it skirts the boundary of the nature reserve.

Follow the track up leaving a farm entrance and a white concrete building on the left. It continues to climb round another right-hand bend past entrances on the right leading to the municipal rubbish tip. Ignore these and continue on the main track as it leads left past a series of small-holdings. It starts to climb again and the alternative route from Molivos enters from the right.
[a5. 21.84'/12.43', 2.83km/1.40km, 25 mins]

Start b. From the starting point *[b1. 39°21.97'/26°10.86']* take the track to the left of the pine wood and follow **Walk 3** to the T-junction with the track from Molivos to the Argenos - Vafios road. *[b4. 21.84'/12.43', 3.00km/1.94km, 35 mins]*

The two starting routes merge here; from now on total distances are from Start a.

The track now runs approximately west-east along the right-hand side of the valley as it rises towards a ridge, which it crosses and continues up the left-hand side of the next valley, with wooded slopes ahead and opposite falling into a stream below.
[6. 21.60'/13.17', 4.20km/1.36km, 15 mins]

As the track bends back to the left after crossing the ridge, go straight ahead to the left of rocks and a metal sheepfold and bear left to follow a path leading diagonally down into the foot of the valley. *[7. 21.47'/13.36', 4.60km/400m, 5 mins]*

Cross the stream and go through the small gate on the far side. Follow the path up through thorn bushes, and where it meets another at a T-junction go right. In five minutes, at a ridge, bear left. The path runs along the left-hand side of a valley, over a small bluff and then down through a small open area and more thorn bushes to another stream.

Cross, go through the gate on the far side and follow the path uphill to an opening into a meadow on the right. (This short stretch is rocky and muddy in places - it doubles as a stream-bed in wet weather).

Follow the path up the left-hand edge of the meadow to the top, then go between rocks into a second field and carry on to its top left-hand corner. Cross a narrow track and go through the gate opposite. *[8. 21.13'/13.27', 5.32km/740m, 20 mins]*

On the right there is a low stone building housing a 'walk-in' water cistern, and diagonally right across the field is the chapel of St John (Αγ Ιωάννις). Walk up through the field to the track at the top and follow it left up to the road at a large single storey white building. *[9. 20.93'/13.43', 5.82km/500m, 10 mins]*

Cross the road and take the track diagonally off to the left (with a green fingerpost ΣΤΑΥΡΟΥΛΑ - ΒΑΦΕΙΟΣ) and follow it uphill to a fork. *[10. 20.72'/13.68', 6.38km/560m, 5 mins]* Go downhill to the right (signed ΒΑΦΕΙΟΣ) and in another ten minutes fork right again. *[11. 20.58'/13.41', 7.10km/700m, 10 mins]* This track leads steeply downhill and in five minutes meets the top of the concrete road into the village. Turn left along the paved street into the village.

In two minutes, at a T-junction, if you intend to continue towards Stipsi turn left uphill and immediately right and walk through to meet the road leading out of the top of the village.

Otherwise turn right and immediately left and walk along to the two cafenions and the church in the village centre. *[12. 20.46'/13.29', 7.40km/300m, 10 mins]*

This is the end of the walk. To return to the main road take the steep downhill street, which rejoins it as it bends downhill by a small playground. The neighbourhood tavernas are a short distance further down the hill.

Molivos to Vafios through Keramotis

Total distance 6.5 kilometres

 Walking time 2 hours 15 mins

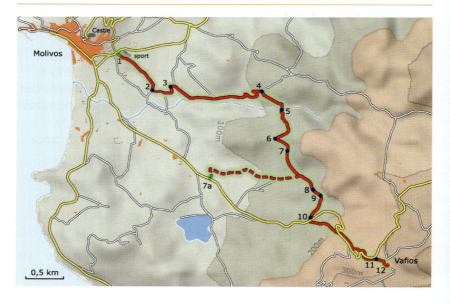

Although the village of Vafios is only six kilometres from Molivos it is comparatively untouched by tourism, apart from the three tavernas on the road which runs below it.

This is a fairly strenuous walk, **part of which runs along a valley occasionally used by the Greek army as rifle ranges, and for occasional artillery exercises. Obviously while firing is in progress it is not possible to walk this part of the route; in any case proceed with caution, and if in any doubt, don't!**

(A sign at the entrance from the Molivos - Vafios road reads ΚΙΝΔΥΝΟΣ ΑΠΟΜΗ ΕΚΠΑΓΕΝΤΑ ΒΛΗΜΑΤΑ ΜΗΝ ΕΓΓΙΖΕΤΕ ΤΥΧΟΝ

ΒΛΥΜΑΤΑ ΕΙΔΟΠΟΙΗΕΤΕ ΣΤΡΑΤΙΩΤΙΚΗ Η ΑΣΤΥΝΟΜΙΚΗ ΑΡΧΗ

"Danger from unexploded shells. Do not touch any shells. Inform the Military or Police Authorities" You have been warned!!).

When firing is in progress it is clearly audible from the town, and should allow you to change your plans if necessary.

From the start *[1. 39°21.97'/26°10.86']*, follow **Walk 3** for the first thirty minutes as far as the farm buildings on the right, then continue on the track as it winds uphill.

In five minutes the track bends sharp left and a secondary track goes off at an acute angle to the right. *[4. 21.71'/12.13', 2.44km/1.40km, 30 mins]* Take this and follow it down to farm buildings in the valley (before it dries up in the summer you will see a small waterfall in the oleander-lined valley below the track). Go round to the left of the buildings and through a small gate on to a path leading diagonally right down to the stream. Cross the stream by the makeshift footbridge. *[5. 21.57'/12.35', 2.94km/500m, 10 mins]* (If you prefer, ignore the gate and bridge

and continue through the farmyard. At the far end cross the stream to join the foot of a track opposite).

If you use the bridge, climb up through the rocks on the far side of the stream and pick up a small goat path leading to the right up the hillside. It soon joins the track - follow this as it winds up the hillside (ignore the branch running off to the left).

The track ends at a fenced field on a ridge. Just before the end go off to the left, along a small path running along the near side of a row of small trees. Wind up through grass and thorn bushes for another five minutes to the head of a gorge. Go left across a rock-face and then diagonally right across a patch of scree. Rejoin the path (it is not always easy to see - keep the farm in the valley directly behind you) and follow it up to a gap on the ridge ahead.

Go over the ridge and across the head of the next valley to the next ridge, cross it near a solitary olive tree, then follow right towards a stone animal shed on the edge of a small pasture.
[6. 21.34'/12.28', 3.44km/500m, 5 mins]

Turn sharp left away from the building on to the path running gently down along the side of the Keramotis valley (below on the right are the ranges). It soon turns right across the head of the valley and ends at a water-trough by a small gate. *[7. 21.27'/12.42', 3.84km/400m, 5 mins]*

Go through the gate and continue on a very faint path for about ten metres, then follow it down to the right. Then turn left on to a wider path leading down along the side of Keramotis to the rifle range in the bottom of the valley, and cross the range to the end of the track opposite (10 mins).

(If you prefer a quicker and easier route to this point, you can walk up the Molivos - Vafios road for about five minutes beyond the beginning of the road leading to the reservoir and Petra, to a track leading off to the left. [7a. 21.06'/11.71'] The warning sign, stencilled black on yellow, is here. Twenty minutes along this track brings you to the end of the rifle range and the point above).

Follow the path leading to the right up the hill behind the target pits. Where it bends right near the top of the field take the smaller path off to the left and follow it up to a gap in the wall. Cross the wall, bear right through a brushwood fence and then immediately left on to a path running downhill. *[8. 20.99'/12.63', 4.56km/700m, 5 mins]*

Follow the path down into a valley. *[9. 20.94'/12.71', 4.74km/200m, 5 mins]* Cross a stream and climb the opposite bank. (The few metres either side of the stream are fairly precipitous, and there is almost always water in the stream - take extra care here). The path continues to climb ahead towards two trees, then bears right leaving a rocky outcrop and tree on the left. Leave another rock and tree on the right, then immediately go between two small trees and head towards the farm buildings visible to the left. Before reaching them the path comes on to the Molivos - Vafios road. The field is fenced along the full length of its boundary with the road, except for a small gap concealed in a thicket of holly-oak just below the farm buildings and directly opposite the bottom of a track on the other side of the road. *[10. 20.77'/12.63', 5.14km/400m, 5 mins]*

(**NB** If you are walking this route from the Vafios end, swing right uphill towards a small ridge after coming through the gap from the road. It is all too easy to follow apparent paths and arrive at the stream at the top of a cliff several hundred metres too far downstream).

Cross the road and take the track (There is a blue sign here 'ΠΡΟΣΟΧΗ ΖΩΑ' - Caution, Animals). Follow this track uphill for ten minutes, with stone walls to the right, until it rejoins the road.

Continue up the road to the right for about 200 metres, and when it swings right at a track signposted ΣΤΥΨΗ 5ΚΛΜ, take the very rough track leading ahead on the left of the road. Follow it round to the left, past a small chapel on the right, and then right to re-emerge on the road at Taverna Ilias (ΤΑΒΕΡΝΑ Ο ΗΛΙΑΣ).

Follow the road uphill until it swings left by a small childrens' playground *[11. 20.49'/13.19', 6.20km/1.06km, 20 mins]*, and then finally take the steep street to the right of the playground up into the centre of Vafios village. *[12. 20.46'/13.29', 6.34km/150m, 5 mins]*

Molivos to Petri

7

Total distance 7.75 kilometres

 Walking time 2 hours 15 mins

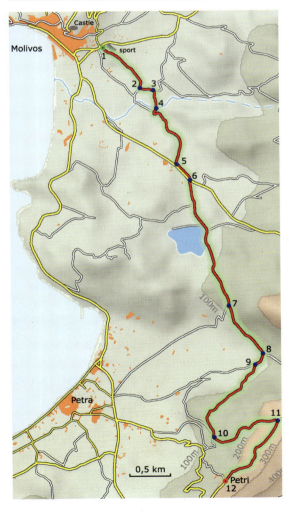

The tiny village of Petri nestles on the north-western end of the Lepetimnos range 260m (850ft) above the sea. The first known record of the village dates from 1602, when it was a mixed settlement of Greek and Turkish families, which it remained until the expulsion of the Turkish population between 1912 and 1923. (In 1909, of 60 households, 10 were Turkish).

Today there are a few holiday apartments, and one or two tavernas, popular for their food and views of the sunset from their terraces, but otherwise little seems to have changed. Despite the tarmac road that now connects the village to Petra, seen from many angles it still appears completely inaccessible.

This is a route that has been affected by road building - about 1½km has disappeared under asphalt since the publication of the previous edition of this book. However at the time of writing the road is incomplete and carries little traffic - as there is no sensible off-road diversion we have retained it unchanged.

From the start *[1. 39°21.97'/26°10.86']*, take the track to the left of the pine wood. Where it divides at a rock face *[2. 21.71'/11.18', 711m, 8 mins]*, turn left over the rise and take the next track to the right. *[3. 21.70'/11.29', 863m/150m, 3 mins]*

Pass through small holdings on the left and orchards and olive groves on the right, and at the next junction bear left. *[4. 21.59'/11.30', 1.07km/210m, 4 mins]* Cross a small river by a concrete bridge, and a little further on go over a small stream where it runs through a culvert. The track rises up through scrubby pasture to the brow of a small hill. Just beyond this a track leads off to the left across a valley; continue along the main track to meet the Molivos - Vafios road to the left of a block of studios. *[5. 21.22'/11.48', 1.87km/800m, 10 mins]*

Turn left on to the road and shortly afterwards take the asphalt road off to the right. *[6. 21.10'/11.59', 2.14km/270m, 4 mins]* It soon passes to the left of the reservoir and begins to climb gently with woodland on the right.

The asphalt road ends at the brow of the hill and becomes a track. Continue downhill until it becomes steeper and bears right, then take the short track leading uphill to the left, and after a few metres turn right through a gate *[7. 20.23'/11.93', 3.62km/1.50km, 25 mins]* (The entrance ahead leads into a quarry).

After about 200 metres pass a long water trough on the left, and in five minutes go through a second gate. In another five minutes the track divides at a small chapel. *[8. 19.95'/12.20', 4.30km/700m, 10 mins]* Take the grassy right-hand track, downhill, cross a riverbed (there is a wooden footbridge), and up, bearing right past a ruined stone building on the bank to the left.

After a few metres go through a gate on the left on to a track running uphill. *[9. 19.89'/12.12', 4.47km/170m, 4 mins]* (A kalderimi continues ahead). Follow the track as it climbs, at first gently and then more steeply, with Petra harbour visible below on the right, through olives, oaks and gradually denser woodland. After leading through several gates (one of these has defeated even us - it can be by-passed by going to the right and over an easily scaled wall), it levels out into open scrubland, and then passes through a final gate to lead gently downhill to a junction with three other tracks. *[10. 19.42'/11.79', 5.64km/1.17km, 20 mins]*

Ahead and to the left is a high volcanic outcrop on the summit of which is a shrine to St Constantine (Αγ Κωνσταντίνος), apparently built on the site of an ancient watchtower of the Classical or Hellenistic period (ie c0-500BC). Take the concrete-surfaced road leading steeply uphill around the foot of the outcrop, with Petri visible to the right on the mountainside opposite. It levels out

briefly, then swings right and climbs very steeply again past cattle-sheds on the right. Soon after this, as the track swings left to cross a ridge, another joins from the right. *[11.19.51'/12.32', 6.61.km/970m, 35 mins]*

Take this, and follow it along the face of the mountain until it enters Petri village. Continue on the main paved street through the top of the village as far as the junction by a post box. *[12. 19.12'/11.87', 7.67km/1.06km, 15 mins]*

You will find welcome refreshment at the village tavernas. You can relax on their terraces with food and drink while deciding where to go next. To visit the church, or return to Petra by **Walk 11**, go down the street immediately on the right past the post box, and down the stone steps at the end. Alternatively, to continue to Stipsi by **Walk 19**, carry on along the paved street past the post box, and down the road to the junction.

Molivos to the Hot Springs of Eftalou and back

Total distance 9.5 kilometers

 Walking time 2 hours 45 mins

*This walk takes you along the cliff tops and beaches to Molivos's neighbouring resort of Eftalou and its medicinal hot springs (At the Eftalou end of the route, about 1km is unavoidably on road). Return inland by a different route, or if you wish continue with **Walk 22** along the shore to the picturesque harbour of Skala Sikamineas. The outward route to Eftalou takes 1½ hours, the return 1 hour 10 minutes.*

The outward route can be a little difficult in a couple of places because of fences crossing the path and continuing into the sea. Be prepared to get your feet wet, and be aware too that in the past the farmer in this area has been obstructive to walkers. Please be especially careful not to give him any valid cause to object to your presence.

The walk begins at Molivos Castle Car Park.
[1. 39°22.11'/26°10.58'].

From the castle car park, follow the road downhill until the first junction. *[2. 22.25'/10.69', 320m, 5 mins]* Turn left on to the dirt road leading to the Pansion Acropol and the hill-top army base, and then almost immediately right on to a path leading downhill. Follow this until it joins the road on a right-hand bend shortly before the Aphrodite and Akti Hotels. *[3. 22.39'/10.88', 785m/465m, 8 mins]*

After the Aphrodite the road continues as a track. Follow it as it leads round the right-hand boundary of the hotel, then turns right uphill and then left again. Continue past a substantial walled development on the right to the end of the track, with the hotel swimming pool and beach below to the left. *[4. 22.66'/11.02', 1.50km/715m, 10 mins]* Turn right along the boundary wall of the property, then continue to the field wall ahead. Follow the rough path left along the line of the wall to the cliff edge, with the solar powered lighthouse to your left. Near the cliff large stones in the wall form a stile. *[5. 22.74'/11.08', 1.69km/190m, 5 mins]*

Cross the wall and fence and go down to a bay and beach. Towards

the far end of the beach a fence extends into the water.
[6. 22.70'/11.27', 2.03km/340m, 10 mins] Go over it or round the end, taking care not to disturb it in any way, and follow the line of the cliff up over the hill ahead. As you climb the coast bends right and Eftalou appears ahead on the left.

Continue for a few metres past a stone animal enclosure until a small path drops down to the left along the cliff-face.
[7. 22.65'/11.43', 2.34km/310m, 6 mins] Follow it down with care - conditions vary but it usually becomes easier as you descend. It meets the sea at the end of a fence. Descend on to the rocks on the sea side of the fence and walk along to the right to reach the beach. *[8. 22.58'/11.47', 2.46km/120m, 8 mins]*

Walk along the narrow beach, passing the ends of two tracks (the first, with a small white-painted fisherman's cottage on the corner, is where the return route diverges) *[9. 22.48'/11.61', 2.73km/270m, 6 mins]*, until it ends at rocks, and a path leads up to the road opposite the ΠΑΝΣΕΛΗΝΟΣ (Panselinos) hotel.
[10. 22.51'/12.01', 3.35km/620m, 12 mins]

Turn left and walk along the road past a fisherman's shack (with, at the time of writing, a resident pack of small, aggressive dogs, which love to loiter on the road and harass passers-by). Continue on the road or along the narrow beach. The road rises to run behind a headland at the end of the bay past the end of a track leading up into the hills on the right.

(This track leads up through a narrow valley for twenty-five minutes to a farm, and then on to the mobile phone mast on the hilltop ahead. From the farm a footpath continues for another twenty-five minutes and finally ends at a hut in an olive grove near a ridge. There is nowhere to go from here but back the way you came, but if you are staying in Eftalou, and want a reasonably gentle morning walk, the wild flowers, particularly in spring, and the views, make this a worthwhile expedition).

Stay on the road over the brow of the hill as it drops down again towards the beach. Directly ahead at the far end of the beach the white dome of the thermal baths is visible. Rejoin the beach and continue to the end, then go back on to the road as it swings uphill to the right. After a few yards a paved track to the baths, which were restored and reopened in the early 1990s, leads off to the left. *[11. 22.72'/12.91', 4.78km/1.43km, 20 mins]*

Follow the path under the cliff behind the modern building which houses administration and treatment rooms and through a doorway into a small tiled lobby. The bath, dimly lit through the ventilation holes in the domed roof, and full of steam from the naturally hot water (43-46°C), is through a low grilled entrance to the left.

Exit on to the beach through the door to the right of the grille and walk along to the taverna perched on the cliff-face overlooking the next bay. *[12. 22.80'/13.06', 5.06km/280m, 5 mins]*

Continue to Skala Sikamineas by **Walk 22**. To return to Molivos climb the steps through the taverna and take the steep concrete driveway up to the dirt road. *[13. 22.76'/13.01',* **distances and**

timings restart from here]

Turn right and follow the road back down to the beach. Retrace your outward route back by the beach, along the road over the headland, and back along the narrow stretch of beach until about 100 metres from the end. Turn left off the beach on a track next to a cottage. *[14. 22.48'/11.61', 2.30km, 35 mins]*

A short distance up the track there is an old Turkish water fountain on the left, followed by the entrance to the Hotel Elpis on the right. When the track forks after this, go right. *[15. 22.43'/11.47', 2.53km/220m, 5 mins]*

Continue uphill through fields, passing large commercial greenhouses, modern houses and apartments. The track continues to the right of the aqueduct tower and leads to a junction with an asphalt road. *[16. 22.28'/11.10', 3.16km/640m, 10 mins]*

Either turn right along the road past Taverna Perikles up to an

acute T-junction. Go left here and at the next T-junction turn right uphill. *[17. 22.17'/10.83', 3.63km/470m, 10 mins]*

Follow this road as it winds up hill until it ends at Molivos Castle car park. *[18. 22.11'/10.58', 4.40km/770m, 10 mins]*

Alternatively, at point 16 turn left on to the asphalt road, and immediately, as the road bends left, keep right to go straight ahead on a narrow track.

This runs between fields and passes a large animal shed on the right, before bending right where a track comes in from the left at a well. *[a17. 22.14'/11.04', 3.42km/260m, 5 mins]* Where it ends at a sloping rock-face bear right up across the rock for about fifty metres and then left to rejoin the path. It leads up between a fenced field on the left and a steep bank on the right to join the Molivos Castle road. *[a18. 22.09'/10.88', 3.70km/280m, 5 mins]* To reach the farmers' co-operative and pine wood turn left on to the road and walk downhill. *[a19. 21.97'/10.86', 3.97km/270m, 5 mins]*

Hills, Valleys, and Sea

Total distance 7.5 kilometres

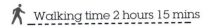
Walking time 2 hours 15 mins

This route is one of contrasts. After climbing along the rugged scrub covered valley behind Molivos, you cross a ridge and descend towards Eftalou across pasture and through the shade of olive groves. Reaching the sea, there is a short stroll along the beach before the final section past market gardens and smallholdings.

NB *At the end of the holiday season (usually in late October/ early November, but sometimes earlier) nets are laid in the olive groves in preparation for the winter harvest. They completely cover the ground, and are easily damaged: therefore this walk is only advisable earlier in the year.*

From the start [1. 39°21.97'/26°10.86'], take the track between the pine wood and the farmers' co-operative and follow **Walk 3** until the T-junction with the track from Molivos to the Vafios-

35

Argenos road. *[4. 21.84'/12.43', 3.00km, 48 mins]*

At the T-junction turn left towards the smallholdings and metal farm buildings that line the left-hand side of the track, but after about 60 metres go through a gate on the right leading towards an older stone farm building, and then immediately right again on to a rough track leading downhill into the valley. *[5. 21.87'/12.41', 3.06km/60m, 1 min]*

Follow this track, keeping right where it forks after about 70 metres, until it begins to level out. Twenty metres before it bends right at a small tree go left on to a faint path. *[6. 21.89'/12.49', 3.20km/140m, 2 mins]* This runs downhill bending left to a stony ridge with a small rocky outcrop on the left. Carry on down the stony path towards the valley. As you get lower it can be difficult to follow, in parts overgrown or obliterated by fire, but go on downhill until you reach a more open area planted with scattered olive and fig trees.

Bear left and head along the valley towards the sea, with several houses visible in the distance. The path (or paths - along this

stretch several sheep-tracks divide and converge but all lead in the same general direction) continues through pasture, across a small stream, and through a gap in a low tumble-down wall.
[7. 22.00'/12.56', 3.50km/300m, 12 mins]

The path is now well-defined once more, leading through a group of oak trees to a track. *[8. 22.06'/12.52', 3.64km/140m, 5 mins]*

Cross the track diagonally to the left and continue on the path opposite, which after two minutes leads through a wall under an oak tree. It divides by more oaks but soon comes together again; the higher, left-hand option is usually easier and clearer to follow. Follow it left under a larger oak and then down right into an olive grove. *[9. 22.14'/12.43', 3.90km/260m, 5 mins]*

Bear left down the terracing, with the stone terrace wall on the right at 1 o'clock (5 mins). Go right and down again, then sharp left round the end of a terrace wall and down another level. Now go right and follow the path downhill to the right through a wall and shrubs - oak on the left, holly-oak on the right.

Immediately bear left and continue down. Go down a steep bank under an old olive tree on to a clear path bearing left through yet more terracing to a level olive-grove below. Continue straight ahead for another five minutes to come out through a brushwood barrier on to the bank of a river (or more likely riverbed, but note that in stormy weather it can become a fierce torrent - another reason for not attempting this walk late in the year) running between stone walls. *[10. 22.29'/12.49', 4.20km/325m, 10 mins]*

Follow the river-bed to the left for about 300 metres until it becomes a concrete road, ignoring the concrete spur leading off to the left. Then continue down the road to join the Eftalou beach road. *[11. 22.49'/12.32', 4.79km/470m, 7 mins]*

Turn left along the road for five minutes, past a fisherman's shack below the edge of the road on the right, and go down the concrete ramp to the beach opposite the Panselinos (ΠΑΝΣΕΛΗΝΟΣ) hotel. *[12. 22.51'/12.01', 5.24km/460m, 5 mins]*

Walk along the narrow beach. Cross the end of one track leading away from the sea, and at the second, by a small fisherman's cottage, turn left. *[13. 22.48'/11.61', 5.84km/600m, 12 mins]*

A short distance up the track there is an old Turkish water fountain on the left, followed by the entrance to the Hotel Elpis on the right. When the track forks after this, go right. *[14. 22.43'/11.47', 6.06km/220m, 5 mins]*

Continue uphill through fields, passing large commercial greenhouses, modern houses and apartments. The track continues to the right of the aqueduct tower. At the next junction *[15. 22.28'/11.10', 6.70km/640m, 10 mins]* turn left on to the asphalt road and immediately, when the road bends left, keep right to go straight ahead on a narrow track.

This runs between fields and passes a large animal shed on the right, before bending right where a track comes in from the left at a well. *[16. 22.14'/11.04', 6.96km/260m, 5 mins]* Where it ends at a sloping rock-face bear right up across the rock for about fifty metres and then left to rejoin the path. It leads up between a fenced field on the left and a steep bank on the right to join the Molivos Castle road. *[17. 22.09'/10.88', 7.24km/280m, 5 mins]* To return to your starting point turn left on to the road and walk downhill. *[18. 21.97'/10.86', 7.50km/270m, 5 mins]*

Petra to Petri or Vafios through the Ligonas Valley (Valley of the Mills)

10

Total distance to Petri 5.75 kilometres: to Vafios 6.75 kilometres

Walking time to Petri 2 hours: to Vafios 2 hours 15 mins

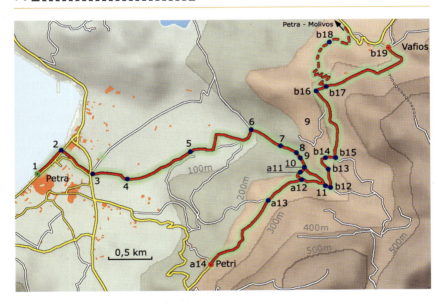

The river gorge running down from the Lepetimnos mountains to the bay of Petra is lined with the massive ruins of mainly nineteenth-century water-mills set amid spectacular volcanic rock formations. The Municipality of Petra has now recognised the historic interest of this valley, and has begun work to encourage visitors: one of the lower mills has been partly restored and information boards, finger-posts, and waymarks erected. There are also descriptive leaflets available from the Petra Tourist Information Office.

A marked trail starts from Petra sea-front (near the football

ground), leads through the lower part of the valley and finishes at Petri. We have adapted the route from previous editions of this book to take account of these and other changes.

From the sea-front square *[1. 39°19.67'/26°10.51'],* walk along the road with the sea on your left, past the bus stop and car park as far as the OTE office. *[2. 19.81'/10.70', 280m, 5 mins]* Take the street to the right of OTE and follow it through the fields to the main road. *[3. 19.68'/10.93', 700m/420m, 8 mins]* Cross the road and take the right-hand of the two roads opposite. This leads through scattered houses for half a kilometre to Petra's identical-twin secondary schools (the γυμνάσιο and λύκειο). *[4. 19.65'/11.22', 1.15km/450m, 7 mins]* It then continues as a dirt road for another 0.8km past a large army apartment block on the right, and then bends sharp right up a steep hill. *[5. 19.79'/11.71', 1.90km/750m, 10 mins]* At this point, leaving a stone barn on your left, continue straight ahead on a broad kalderimi; this degenerates into a track, bends left across a river-bed (there is a wooden footbridge), and leads gently uphill past farm buildings to a small chapel (Ag. Fotia Αγ Φώτια) . *[6. 19.95'/12.19', 2.74km/840m, 15 mins]*

The chapel lies in a V at the junction of two tracks - go past the chapel and through a gate, and turn right to join the other track, which leads uphill through an olive grove as the river gorge deepens on the right. After a stretch of concrete there is a short stretch of paving and a partially reconstructed mill on the left, complete with a helpful explanatory sign-board. Almost immediately afterwards there is the masonry of another ruined mill on the right. As the track begins to level look out for a lesser track leading diagonally up to the left, with a signpost to "ΑΝΩ ΛΙΓΩΝΑ". *[7. 19.86'/12.41', 3.17km/430m, 10 mins]* Take this, and where it doubles back to the left after about fifty metres carry straight on along a path.

This leads above the massive mill-race wall which is all that remains of the next mill. *[8. 19.81'/12.55', 3.41km/240m, 5 mins]* Continue along the narrow path, with an orchard to the left. There is a steel water-pipe, partially encased in concrete, running along the side of the path, which soon comes out at a concrete cistern on the open hillside. *[9. 19.77'/12.57', 3.50km/90m, 5 mins]*

Follow the path up to the left of the cistern along the open hillside above the ravine and the masonry of further mills on both sides of

the valley. It is very faint in some places, paved in others, but runs parallel to the concrete-encased pipeline, and, in places, the original stone channels which fed water to the mills. At a large outcrop on the edge of the ravine to the right of the path there is a small path leading diagonally down into the valley, with a finger-post to 'ΜΥΛΟΙ ΝΟΤΙΑΣ ΟΧΘΗΣ' (Mills on the South Bank). *[10. 19.73'/12.62', 3.62km/120m, 8 mins]* This is an alternative route to Petri giving you the chance to explore the large ruins on the opposite bank of the river. (See Option a below).

Option a: To Petri via the "Mills on the South Bank"

Follow the path as it zig-zags down under the outcrop to the river. Cross the river-bed and go left on to a short kalderimi, leaving the remains of a lower mill building and part of a collapsed masonry chute on your right, to come to the ruined mill house, with the bottom of the water chute and two abandoned mill-stones. *[a11. 19.70'/12.61', 3.75km/130m, 10 mins]* (There were two more mills a short distance upstream on this side of the river, but

their remains are now hardly visible).

There is a broad kalderimi winding away uphill to the right of the mill. Follow it, and when it ends continue up on the rocky path along the edge of the ravine until you come to a track.
[a12. 19.64'/12.59', 4.00km/250m, 10 mins]
Turn right to rejoin the main route to Petri.
(NB Total distances from here are for the main route).

The main route continues ahead past the masonry of another mill race, as the hillside ahead begins to become wooded. The level path ends and turns sharp left uphill for a few metres, and then right on a narrow kalderimi through dense woodland. This part of the route is steep and can become overgrown and slippery.

The path passes the top of another mill, partly hidden in the woodland to the right, and emerges on to a small plateau beyond it with a large rock outcrop resembling a shark's fin to the right.
[11. 19.62'/12.77', 3.90km/280m, 12 mins]

The routes divide here; for Petri follow Alternative a below, for Vafios Alternative b:-

a. Continuation to Petri:
As you face downhill in front of the rock, there is to your left a small path winding down to the stream. There should be blue paint, and possibly red diamond metal waymarks here, but these tend to disappear with time and weather. Go down this path, cross the stream, and climb the opposite bank to rejoin the path. After a few metres it widens into a track leading fairly steeply uphill. Look for a finger-post on the right to "ΜΥΛΟΙ ΝΟΤΙΑΣ ΟΧΘΗΣ" (Mills on the South Bank) at the beginning of a small and inconspicuous path.
[a12. 19.64'/12.59', 4.16km/260m, 8 mins] **Option a.** rejoins the main route here.

Continue up the track to a ridge, with a cattle trough on the left, and a concrete road dropping steeply away to the right.
[a13. 19.51'/12.32', 4.64km/480m, 8 mins]

(For a shorter and easier walk back to Petra, missing Petri, take this concrete road steeply downhill past cattle sheds. It loses its concrete surface, levels out and swings left round the foot of a volcanic outcrop crowned by the shrine of St Constantine (Αγ Κωνσταντίνος). Another steep downhill stretch brings you to a four way crossing. Take the second exit and continue almost straight ahead downhill - this track eventually bends left and brings you back to the Petra secondary schools, from which you can retrace your steps to the beginning of the walk).

Continue on the dirt road ahead to reach Petri. Follow the street as it runs through the top of the village until you reach the junction by the post box (you may have to look for the post box - it is mounted inconspicuously on the right almost behind an electricity pole). *[a14. 19.12'/11.87', 5.68km/1.04km, 15 mins]* The village tavernas are close at hand for refreshments after your exertions. To return to Petra either continue straight ahead past the village car-park, and turn right at the junction to follow the road. Otherwise turn right down the street by the post box and follow **Walk 11** in reverse.

b. Continuation to Vafios:

Continue for a short distance along the path ahead as it leads along the edge of the gorge with the stream on the right. Shortly after a yellow 'Trekking Trail' sign a path comes in at an acute angle from the left *[b12. 19.59'/12.79', 4.00km/100m, 2 mins]*; take this and follow it uphill (it is very overgrown and prickly in places) alongside a rough wall, with views to the left across scrubby woodland to rocky crags.

Continue on the path as it bends to the left *[b13. 19.70'/12.82', 4.20km/200m, 12 mins]*, with a high wall on the right and the crags now ahead. There are views to the left over the Ligonas valley with the track to Petri on the far side. Bear right up the rough stone path to the top of the crag, and right again to follow the path down - in the valley to the left is a group of pale green buildings with a water cistern; a local honey farm. The path zigzags down left and right through a gap in the wall, then up to a gate ahead on the right (ignore a path leading down to the left). *[b14. 19.77'/12.79', 4.44km/240m, 10 mins]* Through the gate a rough track leads up to the Vafios-Stipsi dirt road. *[b15. 19.76'/12.87', 4.55km/110m, 3 mins]*

Turn left on to the road, follow it uphill to the Portas ridge which divides the Petra and Vafios valleys *[b16. 20.20'/12.71', 5.45km/900m, 10 mins]*, then mostly downhill, ignoring side tracks, for another fifteen minutes to reach the centre of Vafios. *[b19. 20.46'/13.29', 6.74km/1.29km, 15 mins]* To return to Petra from Vafios follow **Walk 17**. For a short cut avoiding Vafios; four minutes after crossing Portas take the track leading downhill to the left. *[b17. 20.23'/12.81']* In about five minutes look out for blue waymarks below on the left showing where **Walk 17**, coming uphill from below Vafios, leaves the track *[b18. 20.51'/12.80']*, and follow it from here.

Petra to Petri

Total distance 3 kilometres

 Walking time 1 hour 15 mins

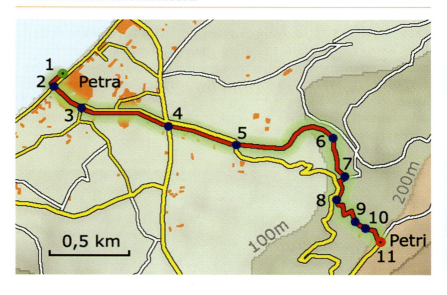

This is a shorter alternative route to the hill-village of Petri, where the terrace of one of its tavernas makes an ideal place for lunch or refreshments.

From the sea front square *[1. 39°19.67'/026°10.51']* take the shopping street to the right (ΟΔΟΣ ΕΡΜΟΥ) running parallel to the beach road behind the Petra Womens' Co-operative guest house and taverna (there is a small local ouzo distillery in this street which is sometimes open to visitors), then turn left into Odos Sapfous (ΟΔΟΣ ΣΑΠΦΟΥΣ - Sappho Street). *[2. 19.64'/10.49', 87m, 2 mins]* Pass the Vareltzidaina mansion and continue under the rock of Panagia Glykofiloussa. Where the street bears left and then right at

a staggered crossing by a small chapel on the right and a mini-market on the left it becomes Odos Nikis (ΝΙΚΗΣ – Victory).
[3. 19.58'/10.61', 297m/210m, 5 mins] Continue along it as it leads out of town to meet the Petra - Kalloni main road.
[4. 19.53'/10.97', 790m/495m, 8 mins]

Cross the main road and take the road opposite sign-posted to Petri (Πετρί). At first the road is level and straight, leading through fields and past scattered houses, but after five minutes it swings right and begins to climb. *[5. 19.46'/11.27', 1.24km/450m, 5 mins]*

At this point follow the track which leads straight ahead, and when, after about 100m, it bears left, keep right on the smaller track leading uphill. This deteriorates into a walled footpath between fields, and for about two hundred metres is also a stream bed.

Continue on the path as it goes right and leads uphill. It eventually turns sharp right at the beginning of a wall (this section can be difficult to follow - look for a red arrow on the wall) *[6. 19.48'/11.68', 1.92km/680m, 20 mins]*, and runs along with the wall on the left. Ignore a path to the right which leads for a few metres down to a water cistern. The path turns sharp left uphill and then right, and passes the ruins, on the left, of an abandoned village - supposedly Turkish, though with a Greek name, Chiliopigada. (This seems to be a corruption of the Greek for Achilles's Wells. According to local legend, Achilles camped here with his army on his way to the Trojan war; in passing capturing and sacking ancient Mithimna).

Cross a rock escarpment to rejoin a faint path between a rock face on the left and a fenced olive grove on the right. Follow along the fence to a small rock-face with a gate on the top. Go through the gate and immediately veer right downhill for a few metres and then left into an olive-grove. Follow along the terraces keeping left up one or two levels until you come to a dirt road. *[7. 19.35'/11.80', 2.26km/340m, 15 mins]*

Turn right on to the road, and descend round a right-hand bend to rejoin the Petra-Petri road. Turn left and follow the road for about

50m, then turn left up a steep concrete drive. *[8. 19.28'/11.68', 2.52km/260m, 5 mins]* This leads between two modern houses (ignore a path leading away above the house on the right), then becomes a rough track which bends left and climbs up to meet a path leading off to the right. *[9. 19.20'/11.76', 2.79km/270m, 8 mins]* This winds uphill, partly on old kalderimi, to emerge at a junction by an apartment block. *[10. 19.16'/11.80', 2.87km/80m, 3 mins]*

Turn left and follow the paved track uphill to Petri church. The church nestles under a cliff at what used to be the foot of the village. (There is a stream flowing under the church - if the church gate is open, it can be seen down steps in the courtyard to the left) Follow the church wall to the right and then go right on the paved and stepped street up into the village. *[11. 19.12'/11.87', 3.04km/170m, 7 mins]*

Petra to Lafionas and return

12

Total distance 7.5 kilometres

 Walking time 2 hours 15 mins

(Outward 65 minutes, return 65 minutes)

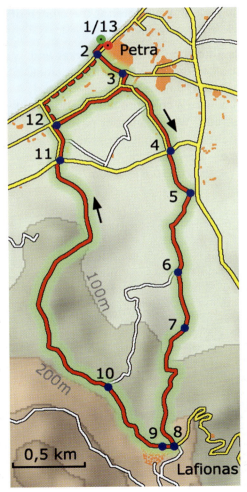

As you come over the ridge from the direction of Kalloni and head down through the hairpin bends towards Petra and the sea below, facing you on the hillside across the valley is the village of Lafionas (Λαφιώνας). Over 200m (650') above the sea, the village stands on a bluff looking down to the coast over two valleys, in a perfect defensive position against pirates, Turks, and tourists alike.

*This walk is a circular route to Lafionas and back from Petra, its half-way point conveniently next to the local taverna in Lafionas. Once at Lafionas you may wish to continue on **Walk 16** to Agios Alexandros, or return via Anaxos by **Walk 15**, but be aware that buses come up here rarely, usually only in early* *morning and mid-afternoon in term-time to ferry local pupils to and from the secondary schools in Petra and Kalloni.*

From the sea front square *[1. 39°19.67'/026°10.51']* take the shopping street (Ermou – ΟΔΟΣ ΕΡΜΟΥ) leading off to the right behind the Petra Women's' Co-operative guesthouse, and then the second street on the left (Sappho – ΟΔΟΣ ΣΑΠΦΟΥΣ).
[2. 19.64'/10.49', 87m, 2 mins] Pass the Vareltzidaina mansion on the left (or go in for a free visit and guided tour) and continue up the street around the foot of the rock on which stands the church of Panagia Glykophiloussa (Παναγία της Γλυκοφιλούσας).

As the street bends left towards a junction by a mini-market and tavernas, take the paved street off to the right in front of a small chapel [3. 19.58'/10.61', 300m/210m, 5 mins], and walk along about 50m to the next junction, where a concrete lane leads ahead. Turn left here on to the paved street. Where another paved street comes in from the left continue ahead on a concrete road (which soon changes to dirt) alongside a watercourse on the left until you reach the "Petra bypass" road. *[4. 19.28'/10.81', 940m/640m, 10 mins]*

Cross the road and take the track directly opposite. Walk between olive groves until you come to a Petra council depot on your left - a wire compound with assorted vehicles belonging to ΔΗΜΟΣ ΠΕΤΡΑΣ. Almost immediately turn on to a track leading off to the right (continuing ahead leads quickly on to the main Petra-Kalloni road). *[5. 19.13'/10.92', 1.25km/310m, 5 mins]* Five minutes later cross a concrete bridge over a stream and begin to climb gently. Lafionas comes into view ahead and above to your right. In another five minutes take a track turning off to the left. *[6. 18.83'/10.86', 1.87km/620m, 10 mins]* Follow it uphill, then at the next junction turn right on to a lesser track. (This track seems little used: parts of it have been washed away by storms and are very rough). *[7. 18.63'/10.88', 2.27km/400m, 5 mins]*

Climb steeply through olive groves for about twenty minutes. (Ignore a smaller track running off to the right into the valley after about ten minutes). As it approaches Lafionas the track runs between stone walls with sections of concrete surface, and then meets the beginning of a paved street. Turn left here on the concrete street over the brow of the hill, which leads immediately to a square with a terrace at the entrance to the village. Here there are seats overlooking the valley, drinking fountain, post box, telephone and bus shelter. *[8. 18.17'/10.84', 3.50km/1.23km, 30 mins]* You will find refreshment here at the taverna ΤΟ ΑΙΘΡΙΟΝ up steps immediately to your right, or at a cafenion on the next corner.

To return to Petra, leave the square by the street on the right, past the cafenion, and follow it round to the right. Pass a church on your right, and a street leading downhill. Immediately after this there is a large cafenion (probably closed; it seems to only open in the evening). Turn right and go downhill under a building that bridges the street. *[9. 18.17'/10.76']* The paved street becomes a concrete-surfaced and then a dirt road as it leads out of the village. When the track divides *[10. 18.40'/10.52', 4.20km/700m, 15 mins]* bear left uphill past a large water-trough on the left.

Follow the track downhill round a right-hand bend then up again round the head of a valley on the right. The sea and Anaxos come into view far below on the left. Continue downhill, passing through walled olive-groves in the lower stages, until the track emerges on to the Petra by-pass road. Turn right along the road, then in about forty metres left at a large fruit and vegetable stall.
[11. 19.25'/10.30', 6.34km/2.14km, 30 mins] Walk down the lane to a staggered crossing. *[12. 19.38'/10.27', 6.60km/260m, 5 mins]*

Here you can go ahead to reach the Petra sea-front road, or turn right and walk along the lane through orchards and market gardens for about five minutes to come back to the junction by the chapel. *[3. 19.58'/10.61', 7.23km/630m, 10 mins]* Turn left and retrace your steps to your starting point. *[13. 19.67'/10.51', 7.53km/300m, 7 mins]*

Petra to Anaxos

13

Total distance 3.5 kilometres

 Walking time 1 hour 15 mins

It is difficult to avoid the main road from Petra to Anaxos, but it can become a bore to walk, especially if you are doing it regularly during a two-week holiday. In particular, the sea-front stretch from Petra square, with coaches squeezing past and a sheer drop into the sea on one side, can induce an acute sense of insecurity.

Here is a much more pleasant route, though as the final stage can involve a scramble over rocks it is not suitable for late night returns from bars or tavernas.

From the sea front square *[1. 39°19.67'/26°10.51']*, take the shopping street (Ermou - ΟΔΟΣ ΕΡΜΟΥ) leading off to the right behind the Kantina bar & Petra Women's' Co-operative guesthouse, and then the second street on the left (Sappho - ΟΔΟΣ ΣΑΠΦΟΥΣ). *[2. 19.64'/10.49', 87m, 2 mins]* Pass the Vareltzidaina mansion on the left (or go in for a free visit and guided tour) and continue up the street around the back of the rock on which stands the church of Panagia Glykophiloussa (Παναγίας της Γλυκοφιλούσας).

As the street bends left towards a junction by a mini-market and tavernas, take the paved street off to the right in front of a small Chapel *[3. 19.58'/10.61', 297m/210m, 5 mins]*, and walk along about 50m to the next junction, where a concrete lane leads ahead. Continue along this lane until the end, then turn right on to the road and walk down to the sea.

As the road swings to the right back towards Petra turn left on to the track along the shore under the cliff. *[4. 19.35'/09.94', 1.63km/1.33km, 20 mins]* (There is a large sign marking the beginning of the Petra - Lapsarna Trekking Trail on the coast road here). Walk along the track, which soon narrows into a footpath along the beach, for about ten minutes, past a couple of beach-side tavernas and a tiny harbour. The island of St George (Νησί Αγ. Γεώργιος) aka Rabbit Island and its smaller companions are offshore to the right. Pass a small plantation of large palm-trees on the left, and also a track winding uphill from the beach.

When the path disappears, carry on along the rocky shoreline for a further five minutes to the next headland, where there are more moorings for small boats, and a gated track leading off the beach. *[5. 19.35'/09.09', 2.96km/1.33km, 30 mins]*

At the next small headland, another five minutes on, pick your way round the end (depending on the state of the water you may have to paddle) or take a moderately difficult scramble on a precipitous path up and over the rocks, (the steps up the cliff to the left lead to a group of private cliff top chalets) and you are at the beginning of Anaxos beach, with its waiting tavernas and sunbeds.
[6. 19.24'/08.97', 3.35km/390m, 15 mins]

Anaxos to Ambelia Beach   14

Total outward distance 2.5 kilometres

🚶 Walking time outward 45 mins; return (by the road) 1 hour

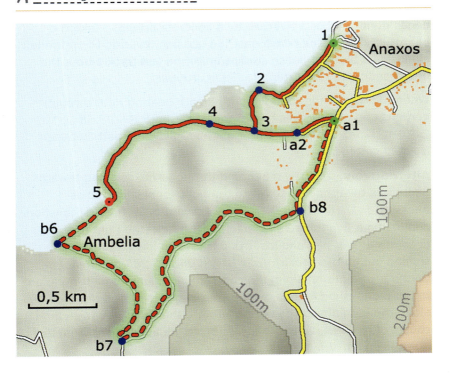

If you have become slightly jaded with the disciplined sunbeds and massed bars and tavernas of Petra and Anaxos, try Ambelia. The shallow bay keeps the sea calm and warm (even by Greek standards), and the beach is clean and under-populated (and naturist-friendly at the Anaxos end), with one small taverna/bar and a river-mouth full of terrapins.

Once upon a time there was a track leading back through the hills to Anaxos, making an almost completely off-road circular route. Unfortunately, from a walker's point of view, this has now become an asphalt and concrete road throughout its entire length.

Start from the Petra end of Anaxos beach.
[1. 39°19.24'/026°08.97']

Walk along the beach, or the road behind it, towards the far south-west end. (The road swings briefly away from the beach, then bends right to cross a riverbed by a concrete bridge). Take the board-walk along the beach past the last fish taverna, then turn left alongside a block of beach studios on to the last track before the beach ends. *[2. 19.04'/08.59', 775m, 10 mins]*

When the track ends continue on the path bearing right through gardens and olive groves to a T-junction. *[3. 18.89'/08.58', 1.10km/325m, 5 mins].* Turn right and follow the path between isolated cottages.

Alternatively:- On the main road through Anaxos going towards Skoutaros take the last street to the right (opposite Studios Anessis). *[a1. 18.93'/08.95']* Carry straight on at the first junction, and in about five minutes keep left at the fork (the right fork becomes a river bed and leads under several low bridges before coming out on the beach). *[a2. 18.88'/08.75', 285m, 5 mins]* Continue straight on along the concrete lane, ignoring a turning on the left, and when it ends, with a small-holding on the right, go on along the path ahead (do not go left into the olive grove). In a couple of minutes, where the route from the beach joins from the right, keep left. *[3. 18.89'/08.58']*

(Indicated distances from here on are from the beach start)

After ten minutes you will pass a low white cottage lying below the path and a path leading off on the left. After another white cottage on the right, the path ends at a gate. *[4. 18.91'/08.35']* Go through the gate and follow the footpath diagonally left across the field towards the cliff top (ignore the path forking right after a few metres). From here the path undulates along the cliff top about twenty metres above the sea. *(In a strong wind, or if you suffer from vertigo, take extra care along this stretch. However it may be reassuring that the locals regularly ride their donkeys along here at a canter).*

The cliff path climbs between walls, passes through a gate and continues along a short steep rocky stretch. It levels out and then begins to descend round the head of a tiny cove with an isolated chapel built above the beach.

After about fifteen minutes drop steeply down and follow the path on to Ambelia beach. *[5. 18.62'/07.85', 2.61km/1.51km, 30 mins]* (If you are returning to Anaxos in this direction, go round left and climb uphill where the path forks just above the beach - do not continue on the path to the right alongside the wall).

Retrace this route to Anaxos, or to return by road, walk to the far end of the beach *[b6. 18.45'/07.57']* and take the concrete road that leads steeply away to the left, marked by a small trekking trail sign. After fifteen minutes come to a T-junction *[b7. 18.01'/07.92']*. The road to the right leads to Skoutaros; turn left downhill past a large building (housing the local laundry) on the left and across the river (more terrapins). The road undulates its way back through the hills and in thirty minutes joins the Anaxos - Skoutaros road. *[b8. 18.55'/08.79']* Turn left along the road and in ten minutes reach the centre of Anaxos.

Lafionas to Anaxos

Total distance 6.5 kilometres

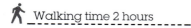 Walking time 2 hours

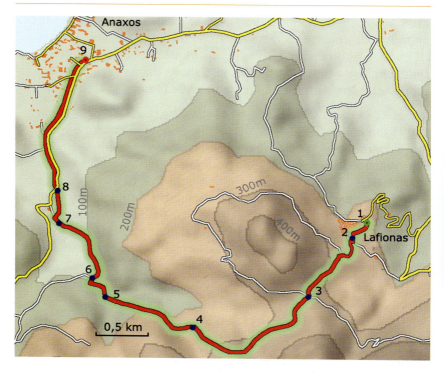

*If you are coming to the end of the circular walk above Lafionas around Roudi and past Agios Alexandros **(Walk 16)** and look to your right down across the valley you will see a tempting track running down through the hills. It winds along the far side of the valley opposite Ag Alexandros through rugged scenery, but also includes a cool shaded glade beside a stream.*

*This description starts from Lafionas, so you can make a circular walk from Petra or Anaxos **(Walk 12)**; but if you are coming from Ag Alexandros or Klapados **(Walk 20)** skip the first section and start from the **.*

From the square at the entrance to the village *[1. 39°18.17'/26°10.84']*, take the left-hand street and follow it round to the wide blue glass-fronted cafenion. Bear left here (there is a sign to Ag Alexandros) uphill to a T-junction. Go left, right at the next T, and where the street forks bear left uphill. All this will take about five minutes.

In two minutes the street starts to lead out of the village. Continue uphill on a concrete road for about five minutes to a T-junction. Turn right up to a parking area *[2. 18.10'/10.74', 360m, 10 mins]*, and then left, still climbing on concrete.

Pass a large water tank on the left - the concrete road becomes dirt about here - to yet another T at the top of the hill. A sign points left to Klapados, right to Ag Alexandros. Go left and climb for another five minutes to another junction. *[3. 17.79'/10.49', 1.20km/840m, 15 mins]*

** Take the right-hand Ag Alexandros track past a water fountain (unfortunately lacking water). Immediately fork left on to a lesser track dropping away downhill, and follow it down into the valley for

about fifteen minutes. At the bottom it crosses a stream-bed, then climbs gently along the side of the valley before heading down again past a roofless stone hut on the right.

Bear left at some large outcrops of white rock *[4. 17.65'/09.75', 2.57km/1.37km, 20 mins]*, and fifteen minutes after crossing the first river arrive at another.

Cross the river bed and follow the track as it climbs up to the right. After fifteen minutes it deteriorates sharply and narrows into a very steep, loose, rough descent leading down to a stream in a narrow wooded valley. (Come in early autumn and this shady area is carpeted with cyclamen). *[5. 17.77'/09.20', 3.41km/840m, 30 mins]* A kalderimi donkey path runs alongside the stream, then crosses it and leads up past a white, blue-shuttered concrete building.

A couple of minutes later the path comes out onto a concrete road. *[6. 17.86'/09.08', 3.95km/540m, 10 mins]* Turning left here will, in twenty minutes and a right turn at the one junction along the way, bring you out on the Anaxos - Skoutaros road about a kilometre below Skoutaros.

For Anaxos, turn right down the steep hill and cross the concrete bridge at the bottom (there are massed oleanders and terrapins in the stream below). Follow the track as it undulates its way gently downhill along the side of the valley with the stream below until it ends. *[7. 18.16'/08.86', 4.69km/740m, 10 mins]*

Continue ahead on a narrow path alongside a stone wall topped with a wire mesh fence, ignoring a path/stream bed leading off to the left after about five minutes. The path is rocky in parts and towards the end becomes a (usually dry) stream bed. It finally turns sharp left and emerges on the Anaxos - Skoutaros road at a culvert alongside a concrete barn. *[8. 18.34'/08.85', 5.05km/360m, 10 mins]*

Turn right and follow the road for 1½ kilometres into Anaxos. *[9. 19.01'/09.07', 6.65km/1.60km, 20 mins].*

If you are not staying in Anaxos, Petra is about 4 kilometres further on foot or by bus following the road, or you can walk down to the beach for a drink or meal, and follow the beach (**Walk 13** in reverse).

61

From Lafionas around Roudi to Agios Alexandros

16

Total distance 4.75 kilometres

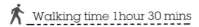 Walking time 1 hour 30 mins

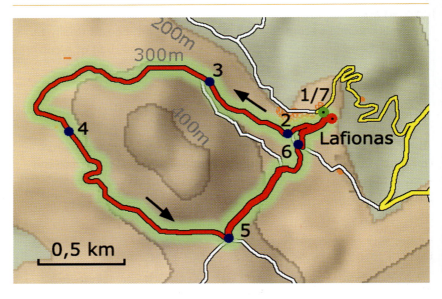

The small mountain (c450m, 1500') which rises behind Lafionas is called Roudi (Ρούδι), or the almost generic name for any high place, Profitis Ilias. On a grassy plateau on its western flank overlooking Skoutaros, surrounded by pine forest and rocky outcrops, are the remains of the early Byzantine (c4th century AD) monastery of St Alexander (Αγ Αλέξανδρος) - medieval Greek monks, like their brothers elsewhere, clearly had keen eyes for desirable locations which would not have disgraced a modern estate agent. In the 17th century the site was occupied by Ottoman colonists who used the stones of the monastery to build their own settlement and mosque. In 1954 the remains of the monastery were discovered

and a small chapel was built on the site. There have been further sporadic excavations since, and some of the remains, an early altar, and carved pediments and capitals from the monastery church, are now housed in the chapel.

A track above Lafionas roughly follows the contour the whole way around the mountain, except for an uphill stretch towards the end, making this a pleasant circular extension of a walk from Petra or Anaxos. (There are picnic tables and a small shelter for a refreshment break at the monastery).

From the square in Lafionas *[1. 39°18.17'/026°10.84']*, take the left-hand of the two streets leading into the village, then almost immediately turn left into a narrow street running downhill.

Follow it as it bends round to the right and then continue uphill, ignoring junctions to right and left, until you reach a T-junction with an old whitewashed fountain in the wall facing you. Turn left and climb steeply up to the next T-junction, and then go right up a stretch of concrete. *[2. 18.13'/10.69', 170m, 5 mins]*

This leads to the left of a house and becomes a narrow kalderimi, with the bay of Petra visible down on the right. Pass a farm building above the path to the left, and then at the fork go left uphill through the trees. After another five minutes the path comes out past a stone chapel and water trough on the right on to a small open plateau. *[3. 18.28'/10.39', 800m/630m, 15 mins]*

Follow the short track that leads up diagonally to the left to join the main track running along the side of the mountain. Turn right on to this track and follow it with the plain of Petra, and later Anaxos, far below to the right. After about twenty minutes, shortly after a rough track leads off down to a rubbish tip on the right, cross a small ridge and Skoutaros comes into view across the wide valley ahead. The track bends down to the left, and soon arrives at the fenced and gated enclosure of Agios Alexandros on the right. *[4. 18.14'/09.83', 2.18km/1.38km, 25 mins]*

From the monastery the track climbs back into the forest (ignore the track forking right just after the monastery: it leads to a promontory with views over the valley towards Skoutaros, but is otherwise a dead end). It continues round the mountain with wooded valleys falling steeply away to the right, then climbs into more open terrain and after about 25 minutes comes to a ridge where there is a seat and a water fountain, unfortunately lacking a water supply. You are now back above Lafionas, facing east, with Petri to the left, and Stipsi visible across the valley ahead. *[5. 17.80'/10.46', 3.60km/1.42km, 25 mins]*

At the junction ahead turn left downhill to return to Lafionas. (The track ahead leads through the abandoned Turkish village of Klapados, site of the final battle to liberate Lesvos from the Turks in 1912, and then on to join the Petra - Kalloni road - see **Walk 20**). Follow down past a large water cistern and trough on the left. At the next fork go right down a steep road, past another cistern on the right, and ignoring a track off to the right shortly after it, to reach a car-park above the village. *[6. 18.10'/10.74', 4.44km/840m, 15 mins]* Go down right again and immediately left into the top of the village. The concrete road becomes a paved street. Turn right at the T-junction, left at the next, and then right again into ΟΔΟΣ ΠΙΤΤΑΚΟΥ. Follow this down to the corner by a cafenion and there either turn left under the building across the street to return to Petra by **Walk 12**, or keep right past the cafenion and church, then follow the street round left to the square. *[7. 18.17'/10.84', 4.80km/360m, 10 mins].*

From Vafios to Molivos or Petra

17

Total distance Vafios to Molivos 6 kilometres: to Petra 5 or 6 kilometres

🚶 Walking time Vafios to Molivos 1 hour 45 mins: to Petra 1 hour 30 mins or 2 hours

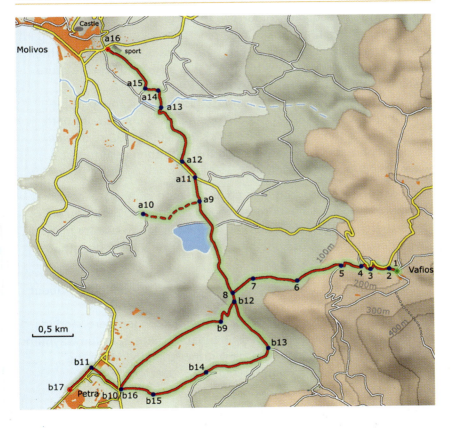

This is one of a small but increasing number of way-marked routes in the Molivos - Petra area. It leads through the hills below Vafios towards Petra to meet the back road from Molivos to Petra.

From Vafios village centre *[1. 39°20.46′/26°13.29′]* take the street downhill to join the Molivos - Argenos road at the childrens' playground on the right. *[2. 20.49′/13.19′, 200m, 4 mins]* Follow the road downhill past the Taverna Vafios and continue as it bends left and right in front of Taverna Ilias (ΤΑΒΕΡΝΑ Ο ΗΛΙΑΣ). In about 100 metres, on a rock on the left of the road, look for a painted blue arrow to Petra (in English) pointing diagonally off to the left. *[3. 20.52′/13.04′, 500m/300m, 5 mins]*.

Follow in the direction of the arrow, then continue down into the valley looking for the blobs of blue paint on rocks alongside the path to mark the way. The waymarked path crosses one track and then meets a second (the 'Vafios bypass' - it is a (just) driveable route leading to the Vafios - Stipsi dirt road). *[4. 20.51′/12.98′, 610m/110m, 4 mins]* Turn left on to this, follow it round to the right and continue uphill for about five minutes until a faint path leads down to the right. *[5. 20.51′/12.80′, 900m/290m, 5 mins]* Go down here for a few metres and the path then resumes at a waymarked rock on the left.

For most of the route from this point the path is unmistakable; there are the occasional unmarked decision points, but in these cases there is invariably a mark within about ten to twenty metres: if you don't come across one by then, go back and try the other option.

However there are two deceptive points worth special note:- about twenty minutes after leaving the track the path forks:
[6. 20.38′/12.42′, 1.52km/620m, 20 mins] keep left here, and in another fifteen minutes turn left up a bank (there is a blue waymark on a rock here if you look carefully) rather than following the obvious path leading straight ahead. *[7. 20.41′/12.06′, 2.08km/560m, 15 mins]*

Most of the way is fairly open, although the path is steep in places. Towards the bottom it becomes narrow and can be overgrown with holly-oak and other thorny vegetation; long trousers are advisable. It finally joins the Molivos - Petra track. *[8. 20.33′/11.91′,*

2.30km/220m, 60 mins from start]

a: For Molivos:- Turn right up the hill on the road leading back to Molivos past the reservoir. At the top of the hill the dirt road becomes asphalt - there is no viable way of avoiding most of this, though once you have passed the reservoir you can take the next clear track to the left. *[a9. 20.95'/11.63', 3.59km/1.29km, 15 mins]* This leads up to the main gate of Karuna *[a10. 20.87'/11.13', 4.42km/830m, 10 mins]*; you can then follow **Walk 4** in reverse back to Molivos.

Alternatively, stay on the road until it joins the main Molivos - Vafios road *[a11. 21.10'/11.59', 3.88km/290m, 5 mins]*, turn left, and then take the next right on to a concrete road that soon reverts to dirt. *[a12. 21.22'/11.48', 4.15km/270m, 4 mins]* Near the brow of the first small hill there is a track to the right leading to a farm. Continue ahead on the main track until it crosses a stream on a concrete bridge and comes to a junction. *[a13. 21.59'/11.30', 4.95km/800m, 11 mins]* Take the track to the right and continue to the next junction. *[a14. 21.70'/11.29', 5.16km/210m, 4 mins]* Turn left, go over the brow of a small hill, and down to the next junction under a rock-face. *[a15. 21.71'/11.18', 5.31km/150m, 3 mins]* Turn right, and follow this track back to the Molivos starting point. *[a16. 21.97'/10.86', 6.03km/720m, 10 mins]*

or b: For Petra. Here again, after a steep downhill stretch of extremely rough hairpins you turn right at the junction at the bottom of the hill *[b9. 20.13'/11.81', 2.79km/490m, 10 mins]*, and after 70 metres come to a dead straight stretch of asphalt road running for 1½km to meet the main road out of Petra towards Kalloni. *[b10. 19.69'/10.95', 4.36km/1.57km, 17 mins]* Cross the road and take the track opposite, which runs across fields to emerge on Petra seafront next to the OTE office. *[b11. 19.81'/10.70', 4.78km/420m 5 mins]* Turn left and walk along to the sea-front square. *[b17. 19.67'/10.51', 5.06km/280m 5 mins]*

For a more interesting, though longer route: about 150 metres downhill from the foot of the path a short spur of track goes left uphill towards a quarry. Take this, but before the quarry entrance go right through a gate *[b12. 20.23'/11.93', 2.50km/200m, 5 mins]* and follow the track, passing a long water-trough on the left and going through another gate.

Fork right at a chapel (Ag. Fotia – Αγ Φώτια) *[b13. 19.95'/12.19', 3.20km/700m, 10 mins]* (continuing ahead takes you to Ligonas, the valley of the mills, see **Walk 10**), drop slightly downhill, crossing a stream by a footbridge, and follow the track round to the right. After a gate on the left the track becomes a wide kalderimi, which leads down to a dirt road. *[b14. 19.79'/11.71', 4.04km/840m, 14 mins]* Go straight ahead, past a military apartment block on the left, to Petra's two secondary schools, the γυμνάσιο and λύκειο *[b15. 19.65'/11.22', 4.79km/750m, 10 mins]*, where the asphalt road begins. Follow this to the main road. *[b16. 19.69'/10.95', 5.24km/450m, 5 mins]* Cross the road and finish on the route above. *[b17. 19.67'/10.51', 5.94km/700m 10 mins]*.

Vafios to Stipsi round the Mountain   18

Total distance 6.25 kilometres

 Walking time 1 hour 30 mins

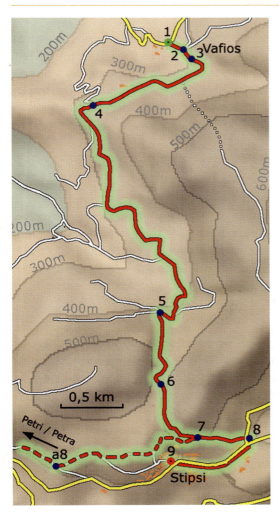

Once you have walked to Vafios you will probably want to go on. This walk leads up and around the end of the Lepetimnos range before descending into Stipsi on the southern face of the mountain. From Stipsi return by taxi, or if you are still feeling energetic continue walking and return via Petri.

Start on the main road from Molivos where it bends left by the bus shelter near Taverna Vafios. [1.39°20.49'/26°13.19'] Walk up the steep paved street leaving a small childrens' playground on the left. In a couple of minutes follow the street as it bends right between the village church on

the right and one of the two village cafenions on the left.
[2. 20.45'/13.29', 162m, 3 mins]

Continue up this street, and follow it as it then leads downhill out of the village. (If you are continuing from **Walk 5**, the street through the top of the village joins from the left near the brow of the hill). *[3. 20.43'/13.33']* Ignore a tempting trekking trail sign and blue fingerpost (To Prophet Ilias) pointing up stone steps to a footpath on the left.

The street becomes a concrete road bending right around the end of the valley with a trekking trail sign on a tree to the left at the apex of the bend. Follow the road as it leads uphill and becomes a dirt track. There are views right across Vafios to Molivos until the track crosses the ridge (this pass is known locally as 'Portas' - the gate (Πόρτας) and bends left into the next valley to give vistas over Petra, Anaxos, Lafionas and across to (yet another) Profitis Ilias to the north of Skalachori. *[4. 20.20'/12.72', 1.46km/1.30km, 17 mins]*

Continue up the left-hand side of a wooded valley with walled and gated orchards and olive groves on the right. The track eventually reaches the head of the valley and hairpins right, leaving a locked gate and track to the left. Continue steeply uphill on the main track and at the next left-hand hairpin continue to the left, ignoring tracks leading straight ahead and to the left (the latter leads to an experimental thermal energy installation). *[5. 19.32'/13.16', 3.87km/2.41km, 35 mins]*.

Carry on upwards past modern farm buildings on the left and water troughs on the right, again ignoring the tracks on the left and right, to arrive at a whitewashed stone circle on the left housing a old circular shrine. Behind it is a much newer chapel and campanile, with the dedication ΔΑΠΑΝΗ ΜΑΙΡΗΣ Ε ΜΩΥΣΗ 1998.
[6. 19.00'/13.15', 4.59km/720m, 15 mins] At about 460m (1500ft) this is the highest point of the walk; from here it is downhill all the way to Stipsi, and behind the chapel is a walnut tree where, provided you haven't already emptied your water-bottle, you can

celebrate with a drink in the shade.

Continue to follow the track as it descends through fields. Stipsi is one of the centres of the Lesvos honey industry, and depending on the season you may pass beehives as well as pasture and arable land. Ahead there are views over central Lesvos down to the salt-pans of the Gulf of Kalloni, before Stipsi itself comes in to view on the hillside below.

A track soon leads off to the right - this runs along above Stipsi and leads on round the end of the mountain range and down to Petri **(see Walk 19)**. *[7. 18.77'/13.36', 5.24km/650m, 9 mins]*

If you wish to continue to Petri without visiting Stipsi take this track as it undulates along above the town. There are a number of concrete streets leading downhill into the centre should you change your mind about visiting. After twenty minutes and 1.5km the track finally leads steeply downhill on a stretch of concrete, which ends just before a junction with two tracks going off to the right (by an open-sided barn housing refrigerated milk collection tanks), and one coming up from the left. *[a8. 18.639'/12.574']* Take the second track on the right to join the route to Petri.

Continuing on the main route brings you to the road from Stipsi along the southern flank of the mountain range to Ypsilometopo, Pelopi and Kapi, near the junction with the Stipsi bypass. *[8. 18.79'/13.61', 5.64km/400m, 7 mins]* Turn right, and then immediately follow the road round to the right, passing the sports ground on the left, into the centre of Stipsi. *[9. 18.68'/13.24', 6.24km/600m, 10 mins]* There are shops, cafenions, and a drinking fountain (dated 1992, and donated according to the inscription by the Stipsian Association of Athens – ΔΩΡΕΑ ΣΥΛΛΟΓΟΥ ΣΤΥΨΙΑΝΩΝ ΑΘΗΝΑΣ) - this is still very much a traditional Greek country town where everything, apart from the cafenions, closes in the afternoon. If you want to explore, much of the town lies on the side of the mountain below the main street: in fact the slope is so steep that the car park at the far end of the main street is built on the flat roof of the olive oil factory below.

The road leads west out of Stipsi towards the other end of the bypass and the junction with the Petra - Kalloni road. On the left, behind the village school (ΔΗΜΟΤΙΚΟ ΣΧΟΛΕΙΟ ΣΤΥΨΗΣ) there is a rocky outcrop on the left crowned by the chapel of St George (Αγ Γεώργιος), with its bell hanging under a bright blue canopy. The chapel is normally closed, but its terraces give panoramic views over Stipsi and the Lepetimnos range, across the central plain to Kalloni, and to the west to the hills of Klapados **(see Walk 20)**. To reach the chapel, take the concrete path to the left of the school and continue between the white marker stones through the pine-wood and up the steps.

Then decide whether to continue home via Petri **(Walk 19)** or return to the village for a drink, a meal, and a taxi.

Petri to Stipsi   19

Total Distance 4.5 kilometres

 Walking time 1 hour 15 mins

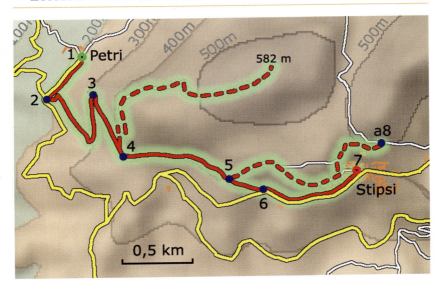

This route climbs round the end of the mountain range behind Petri, with views across the valley towards Lafionas. For anyone with an urge to get to the top of the mountain (known variously as Mt Stipsi, or Roussa (Ρούσσα) depending on the map), there is a diversion, with, on the way, an 'aerial' panoramic view of the north Lesvos coast from Cape Petinos to Eftalou and beyond.

Start in Petri at the T-junction by the post box on the main street across the top of the village. [1. 39°19.12'/26°11.87']   Follow the road downhill out of the village past the small parking area and the ruins of the old village school to the junction.
[2. 18.98'/11.71', 660m, 10 mins]

73

Turn left, then immediately sharp left again uphill on to a track. This bends left, then right, heading south. Ignore a minor track coming in from the left, and another leading temptingly off to the left through an oak plantation when the main track bends sharp right. *[3. 18.98'/11.93', 1.65km/990m, 20 mins]* (There may be a gate across the track at this junction - if you are coming from Stipsi be careful not to miss it - it is all too easy to follow straight ahead on the obvious track and five minutes later find yourself at a dead end).

Now stay on the main track as it continues to climb south along the edge of the valley, with the village of Lafionas visible on the opposite hillside, resisting the temptation of two minor tracks plunging down to the right.

Eventually the track bends left round the end of the ridge. The Stipsi road appears below on the right: a track runs off uphill to the left of a white barn, cistern and water-trough. *[4. 18.73'/12.09', 2.53km/880m, 10 mins]*

(This track leads back up round the end of the ridge to the transmitters on the summit above Petri, on the way giving an unrivalled view over Petri and the Petra plain down to the sea. When the track ends at the masts, leave it and curve back above the main antenna, looking for a gate in the stone wall on the right. Go through this and continue uphill, keeping the wall on your left. The summit (582m) is marked with a concrete surveying post - if you can spot this it makes a useful target to aim for. Retrace your steps to rejoin the main route).

To continue to Stipsi walk on along the main track, parallel to the road below. It leads through a farm, and then reaches a junction. *[5. 18.64'/12.57', 3.32km/790m, 10 mins]*

If you wish to continue to Vafios on **Walk 18** without going into Stipsi, follow the alternative route below, otherwise take the right-hand track which runs downhill on a short, steep stretch of concrete for five minutes to join the main road at the entrance to the town near the school. *[6. 18.60'/12.78', 3.65km/330m, 5 mins]*

Turn left to walk into the town. After a few metres there is a modern (1993) drinking fountain on the left. On the right a little further on is the primary school, and on a rocky mound in a pine wood behind is the chapel of St George (Αγ Γεώργιος), with its bright blue campanile. To reach it take the path leading down to the right in front of houses a few metres after the school and follow it through the trees surrounding the mound.

The road leads to the main street of Stipsi, with cafenions and some small shops. *[7. 18.68′/13.24′, 4.35km/700m, 15 mins]* Much of it lies on the steep hillside below the road - the car park that you pass on your right as you enter the town is the flat roof of the local olive oil factory.

Alternative link to Walk 18:- Go uphill on the left-hand track and bear right, ignoring a track off to the left. The track runs along the side of the hill above the town. If you continue to the end, and turn left, you will be on the track back over the mountain to Vafios **(Walk 18)**. *[a8. 18.77′/13.36′, 4.80km/1.48km, 25 mins]* However if you change your mind and decide to go into the town there are several side tracks and paths leading off downhill, any of which will eventually lead down to the main street.

A Forest Walk to Klapados and Lafionas

20

Total distance 7.25 kilometres

 Walking time 2 hours 30 mins

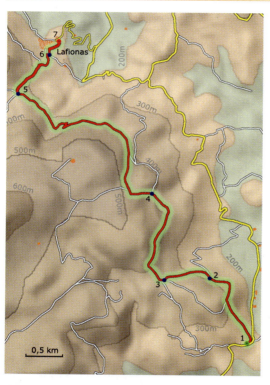

This walk follows a forest trail along the hillside overlooking the central valley of Lesvos, passing through the ruined Turkish village of Klapados, site of the final battle between the Greek and Turkish armies in 1912 which liberated Lesvos from 450 years of Turkish rule. There are benches and occasional picnic tables at particularly scenic points along the way, and plenty of shade from the trees.

The easiest way to reach the start of the walk is to take the Molivos - Mitilini service bus. When you get on ask the driver or conductor to put you down at the road to Klapados. After crossing the ridge at the end of the Lepetimnos mountain range behind Petra, the road drops down past the junction for Stipsi, and winds its way along the hillside. After about five kilometres the road swings right into the forest before beginning its descent to the plain of Kalloni. On this bend there is a forest road off to the left, and immediately afterwards another rising sharply to the right with an 'Ecological Route' sign-board at the junction. Get off here.

Walk up the track past the sign *[1. 39°15.90'/026°12.64']*. After climbing for about fifteen minutes, with views to the right across the valley towards Stipsi, the track levels out and branches, with a subsidiary running off downhill to the right towards the road below *[2. 16.39'/12.28', 965m, 20 mins]*. It then continues uphill again, heading approximately west.

It finally reaches a crest, with views down to the left to the Gulf of Kalloni *[3. 16.37'/11.84', 1.65km/690m, 10 mins]*. Ignore the track that branches off downhill in that direction, and continue on the main track as it climbs again, round to the right back into the forest, with a walled orchard and stone hut on the right.

In five minutes you reach a level grassy area on the left. Go on uphill past a water cistern on the next right-hand bend and continue to climb gently northwards. Ignore the rough track leading diagonally off uphill to the left after another ten minutes; just beyond here there is a viewpoint on the right looking across the valley towards Stipsi, Pelopi, and the Lepetimnos mountains. This is more or less the highest point of the walk, and a good place for a rest to admire the view.

The track now begins to descend. It bends left and continues downhill, with the ruins of Klapados visible on the hillside ahead. As you approach the track bends to the right and leads along the foot of the village. Near a sign commemorating the battle there are the domed remains of the village bathhouse, by a spring which now feeds a new water-trough *[4. 17.09'/11.75', 3.27km/1.62km, 30 mins]*. Above it is a giant plane tree, still alive despite having been struck by lightning and almost destroyed by the resulting fire.

Carry on up out of the village and curve left to head west on the level again. Pass a cistern on the left, and follow the track round to the right and up again, ignoring side tracks down to the right and left.

In five minutes start to descend, with Petra, Molivos Castle, and the Turkish coast visible through the trees ahead. Carry on for fifteen minutes, then cross a cattle grid and continue down to a right-hand hairpin bend by a water fountain dated 1998 (which may or may not be connected to its water supply). This is quickly followed by a left-hand hairpin, and a right-hand bend leading over a concrete bridge and across the head of a valley, until in another fifteen minutes you reach the junction above Lafionas. *[5. 17.79'/10.49', 6.05km/2.78km, 1 hr]*

Take the right-hand track, signed Λαφιώνα - Lafiona and follow down past a large water cistern and trough on the left. At the next fork. go right down a steep concrete road, past another cistern on the right, to a car-park above the village. *[6. 18.10'/10.74', 6.90km/850m, 15 mins]* Go down right again and immediately left into the top of the village. The concrete road becomes a paved street. Turn right at the T-junction, left at the next, and then right again into ΟΔΟΣ ΠΙΤΤΑΚΟΥ. Follow this down to the large cafenion (see **Walk 12**) and from there return to the square *[7. 18.17'/10.84', 7.26km/360m, 10 mins],* or bear left downhill to continue to Petra.

A Circular Walk from
Skoutaros to Tsichrada

21

Total distance 6.5 kilometres

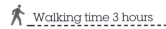 Walking time 3 hours

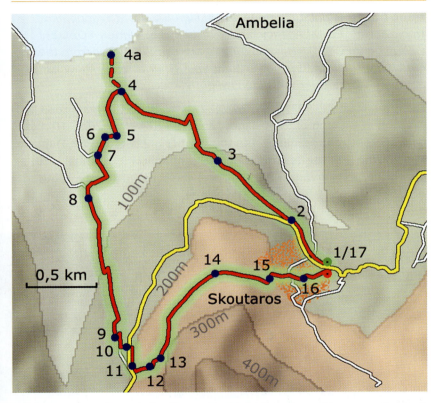

Skoutaros is a large hill village, about 200m above the sea, situated at the head of the valley running down to the beaches of Tsichrada (Τσιχράντα) and Ambelia (Αμπέλια). It is the 'parent' village of Anaxos (which was originally called Anaxos Skoutarou), most of whose holiday properties, tavernas and shops are owned and run by

Skoutaros residents, and so is one of the few villages in Lesvos whose population is lower in summer than winter.

Surrounded by varied olive groves, woodland, and agricultural land, and with unrivalled views down to the coast and across to Turkey, it is the ideal starting place for this scenic walk.

The walk starts on the main road through the village, at the foot of the first main street leading up to the left, and measurements are taken from this point (there is a blue sign here to 'Ταχυδρομικό Πρακτορείο - Postal Agency' and a rusty street name – "ΟΔΟΣ ΘΕΜΙΣΤΟΚΛΕΟΥΣ"). However if you are coming by car from the direction of Anaxos it is easier to drive further through the village and park where the road widens slightly.

From the start *[1. 39°17.50'/26°08.11'],* walk up the main road to the sign at the end of the village. *[2. 17.68'/07.95', 420m, 10 mins]* Take the dirt road leading off to the right (signposted 'Προς Παραλία Τσιχράντας – To the Tsichrada Beach), and follow it downhill, with views over to Molivos on the right and the coast of Turkey in the distance ahead.

Pass farm buildings on the right, and then a chapel on the left. *[3. 17.91'/07.61', 1.07km/650m, 10 mins]* Continue down the hill towards the bay of Tsichrada – its houses dotted along the beach and in the valley behind are now in sight.

After twenty minutes a small path leads off to the left alongside a fence. *[4. 18.18'/07.13', 2.12km/1.05km, 20 mins]* The walk goes this way, but to reach the beach continue down the dirt road for another 350m. *[4a. 18.33'/07.09']* The road turns left along the beach towards two tavernas, crossing a stream on the way, while at the end of the beach to the right, nestling under cliffs, there is another chapel with a terrace which is ideal for a short break.

From the junction at *[4]* the path runs beside the fence, then along a stream. After five minutes, where the stream comes in from the left, keep right up the path (depending on the season this may also be a lesser stream). The path bends right *[5. 18.01'/07.14', 2.44km/320m, 15 mins]*, up a short stretch of kalderimi leading through a gate into a farm. *[6. 18.02'/07.08', 2.57km/130m, 5 mins]* (Be sure to close this gate securely – the farmer lives nearby and may be watching you!)

Turn left on to a track for a short distance to a concrete road. *[7. 17.92'/07.02', 2.77km/200m, 2 mins]* Go left and continue to the next T-junction, ignoring a concrete track coming in from the left. *[8. 17.78'/06.98', 3.09km/320m, 5 mins]*

Turn left on to the dirt road and follow it as it zig-zags uphill. At the last right-hand hairpin bend, just before the surface becomes concrete, take a small path to the left. *[9. 17.27'/07.16', 4.36km/1.27km, 20 mins]* The path leads to the small chapel of Agia Marina, with another pleasant terrace where you can rest after your climb and enjoy the view back down to the sea.

From the chapel follow a kalderimi uphill for a few metres, and when it ends go left up a rough path to reach the main road from Skoutaros to Filia and Skalochori. *[10. 17.26'/07.21', 4.46km/100m, 5 mins]*

If you wish you can turn left here and follow the road for just over

2km back to Skoutaros. However to continue the walk turn right along the road until you come to a concrete ramp on the left leading up to an olive grove. *[11. 17.16'/07.18', 4.67km/210m, 5 mins]* Go into the olive grove (you may have to climb the fence to the left of the gate), and work your way up the terraces, trying to keep diagonally left, until you come to a narrow path running along a terrace. This will probably take about ten minutes: take your time as it is easy to miss your way on this section. Follow the path to the left as far as the corner of a field surrounded by a rusty wire mesh fence. *[12. 17.21'/07.31' 4.96km/290m, 15 mins]*

Follow along the fence as it bends right. A few metres later it goes left again; follow the wire netting fence which joins it and continues ahead for a few more metres. Where the fence ends at a large olive tree climb over the wall to the left and join a clear path ahead. *[13. 17.22'/07.35', 5.16km/200m, 5 mins]*

Continue on this level path (after a few metres the rusty wire mesh fence comes up to run alongside it for a while) until it reaches an animal shed on the left. *[14. 17.53'/07.61', 5.62km/460m, 20 mins]* It climbs briefly between walls, then levels out with a view of Molivos ahead in the distance, and descends once more to another animal shed. Petra and Anaxos come into sight below.

Go on past more animal pens and sheds until the path ends at the top of a short track. Follow the track down to a junction. *[15. 17.50'/07.84', 6.16km/540m, 20 mins]* Turn sharp left down a steep concrete street to the next crossing; sharp right downhill again, then straight ahead at the next junction. Take the next left turn down paved steps, and at the bottom turn right and immediately left. Bear right to arrive at Skoutaros church. *[16. 17.49'/08.00', 6.41km/250m, 10 mins]*

Go down the steps to the left of the church, turn right and left past the village school, then take the second street running downhill to the left (with a sign 'To Center') to return to the starting point on the main road. *[17. 17.50'/08.11', 6.64km/230m, 10 mins]*

Eftalou to Skala Sikaminias

22

Total distance 9.5 kilometres

 Walking time 2 hours

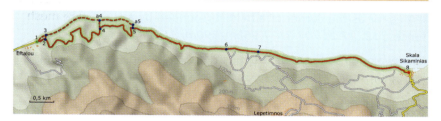

*This walk continues from the Eftalou end of **Walk 8**, and takes about another two hours, making Molivos to Skala Sikaminias an ideal morning's walk if you are feeling energetic. Apart from the taverna by the thermal baths at Eftalou, there is another along the way, near the halfway mark, and plenty of opportunities to pause for a refreshing swim, perhaps in the fresh-water hot spring under the sea near the half-way point. Arrive at Skala Sikaminias in time to explore the village, centred round its picturesque harbour, and have lunch at one of the harbour-side tavernas, then return to Molivos by boat in mid-afternoon. (There is a daily excursion boat during the holiday season, and one-way tickets are usually available at the boat in Skala Sikaminia, or from the travel office at the Seahorse Hotel on Molivos harbour).*

Note that some maps and signs shorten Sikaminia (Συκαμινιά) to Sikamia (Συκαμιά) or Skamia (Σκαμιά); the place is the same.

NB: Main distances and timings are for the road route.

Start from the end of the paved road leading to the thermal baths *[1. 39°22.72'/ 026°12.91']* and walk up the steep dirt road as it zig-zags uphill. A road leading precipitously down on the left leads to a beach tavern. *[2. 22.76'/13.01', 240m, 5 mins]*

(During the holiday season you can also walk on along the beach from the baths, and through the rocky outcrops on the headland to the taverna on the next large beach. *[3. 22.80'/13.06', 280m, 5 mins]* Climb the steps through the taverna and up its steep entrance drive to the road *[2]*. At the junction turn left uphill).

Alternatively, you can continue along the beach from the taverna to the headland at the far end, and then through a series of small bays under the cliffs. The beaches change radically depending on winds and tides, particularly at the ends of each bay where the cliffs approach the water, and getting from one to the next may involve a certain amount of wading or easy scrambling over rocks - be prepared to get your feet wet. Note also that the bays are secluded and therefore predominantly naturist; don't come this way if you are easily shocked by naked flesh.

The cliffs eventually give way to meadows sloping up to the dirt road which here drops back towards the shoreline having led over and behind the headland. Halfway along this beach, by a water-trough *[a4. 22.98'/13.80', 895m/615m, 25 mins]*, a rough track leads up to join the road *[4. 22.87'/13.80', 1.08km/185m, 5 mins]*, but if you prefer continue along the beach, and around the next low

headland. Finally cross a river-bed running across the beach, and immediately take the short track for 100m *[a5. 22.93'/14.28', 1.65km/755m, 15 mins]* up to the road. *[5. 22.89'/14.26']*

The road route climbs round the head of a valley then leads over a headland and downhill to the right and then left back towards the sea past a small block of holiday studios in the next valley.

After the studios the road bends right to run parallel with the sea, and passes the head of the first track running down to the beach. *[4. 22.87'/13.80', 2.33km/2.09km, 20 mins]* Follow it as it continues to wind along the coast, sometimes at sea level with fields and olive-groves on the right stretching back to the foothills of the Lepetimnos range, sometimes rising through woodland over rocky headlands. From time to time tracks head off the road towards the hills; ignore these.

There is a tiny beach taverna, in a fisherman's cottage, after forty minutes, immediately before a concrete road (doubling for a few yards as a riverbed) *[6. 22.66'/15.59', 5.70km/3.37km, 45 mins]*

leads away into the hills, the 'new' village of Lepetimnos, and the Sikaminia - Argenos road.   Carry on along the shore and pass a small chapel (St Dimitrios –Αγ Δημήτριος) as the road starts to rise again. *[7. 22.63'/16.04', 6.30km/600m, 10 mins]*

Finally, the road becomes surfaced and leads into Skala Sikaminias harbor. *[8. 22.42'/18.18', 9.53km/3.23km, 40 mins]* The harbour is lined with fish tavernas which at weekends are favourite destinations for Greek family parties, and there is no better place to relax with a beer and a meal while waiting for the boat back to Molivos.

Skala Sikaminias is also famous for the harbour church of Our Lady of the Fishermen (Παναγία των Ψαράδων), better known as the Mermaid Madonna (Παναγία της Γοργόνας), so named, it is said, from a wall painting of the Virgin Mary with a mermaid's tail. (The picture no longer exists, if it ever did; the current wall paintings were all done in 1992. It is possible that the story had no reality except in the novel 'The Mermaid Madonna' by the famous local author Stratis Mirivilis, which was set here - it may or may not be significant that while the novel, which was published in the 1950s, is set in the period of the Anatolian Catastrophe of the early 1920s, a painting of Skala Sikaminias by the naive painter Theophilos dated 1933 does not show the church at all).

Skala Sikaminias to Sikaminia circular routes

23

Total distances:

Outward 2.5 kilometres

Return via route a 7.5 kilometres, route b 9.25 kilometres

🚶 Walking time:

Outward: 1 hour, Return via route a 2 hours 15 mins
route b 2 hours 45 mins

Walking the road from Skala Sikaminias to Sikaminia is hard work and discouraging even to enthusiastic walkers like us. Apparently never-ending hairpin bends seem to bring you no nearer to the village high above you. (Going down is different, of course, and has the bonus of continuous sea views across the strait).

This route, on the other hand, for much of the way follows one of the original cobbled kalderimia which until well into the 20th century were the main thoroughfares between the two villages.

Although fragmented by new tracks that have been bulldozed across the sides of the mountain, much of it still survives in good condition. Unfortunately, nothing can alter the fact that while the two villages are less than 1½ kilometres apart as the crow flies, one is 300m higher than the other.

In theory fast walkers should be able to take the morning excursion boat from Molivos or Petra to Skala Sikaminias and complete one of the walks here in time for its afternoon return. In practice you will probably want to explore the harbour and the neighbouring beaches, and still have time for a meal in one of the fish tavernas, so will prefer to come by car or taxi.

Leave the harbour at Skala Sikaminias *[1. 39°22.42'/26°18.18']* along the concrete sea-side road leading towards Eftalou, and continue as far as the rocky outcrop surmounted by the former restaurant-bar Medusa (ΜΕΔΟΥΣΑ). *[2. 22.46'/17.99', 300m, 5 mins]* Turn left here on to a track leading uphill away from the sea. A green fingerpost points to ΚΟΥΦΟΒΟΥΝΟ & ΠΛΑΤΑΝΙΑ ΓΛΥΝΑΔΟΣ. (The Medusa has closed down, but at the time of writing its sign is still on the white entrance arch at the foot of the rock).

The track bends right by a small radio mast; shortly afterwards turn left at the next junction *[3. 22.35'/17.81', 665m/365m, 5 mins]*, and follow up past water-tanks on the left. After a few minutes there are two junctions in quick succession: keep right at the first, and at the T-junction immediately afterwards, with a river-bed ahead, cross diagonally to the right and go up the bank on to a path through an olive grove. *[4. 22.22'/17.82', 945m/280m, 5 mins]* The path crosses the river and continues on the other side as a walled kalderimi. It soon comes to a T-junction *[5. 22.20'/17.79', 1.04km/100m, 5 mins]*; turn right and follow the kalderimi uphill with a wall on the left.

At the next junction turn left uphill again on the kalderimi. *[6. 22.18'/17.77', 1.08km/40m, 2 mins]* (The path straight ahead here leads immediately to a level area by a stream - a pleasant spot if you are ready for a break). The route continues uphill on a mixture of kalderimi, loose stone, and earth, for about five minutes, then bends left for a few metres with a stream bed on the right before continuing up on a stepped kalderimi to join the bottom end of a track at the gates of two fenced olive groves. *[7. 22.07'/17.75', 1.34km/250m, 5 mins]*

Turn right on to the track and follow it uphill for about 120m, with the stream below on your right. Ignore a track leading off to the left. At the brow of the hill *[8. 22.01'/17.73', 1.44km/100m, 5 mins]*, go sharp left up a steep rocky path, which leads back on to kalderimi. This zigzags right and left uphill, followed by a level stretch along the top of an olive grove. It then turns uphill again for a short distance, turning sharp right where it meets the foot of a concrete water channel. *[9. 21.98'/17.82', 1.58km/140m, 5 mins]* (The water should go off to the left here, guided by a makeshift dam, but in wet weather will probably use the path you have come up as an alternative route).

Continue uphill on kalderimi to meet another track.

[10. 21.95'/17.79', 1.71km/130m, 3 mins] Turn sharp right on to this and follow it up through three sharp bends until its junction with a wider track. *[11. 21.90'/17.81', 1.96km/250m, 7 mins]*

Go right again, climb for 5 minutes and then, about 100m before the brow of the hill, rejoin the kalderimi alongside a wire fence on the left *[12. 21.82'/17.72', 2.20km/240m, 5 mins]*. A final climb, keeping left on the kalderimi where a rough path leads ahead, leads up to a short stretch of crumbling concrete path, and brings you to the narrow main road running round the foot of Sikaminia village. *[13. 21.75'/17.75', 2.35km/150m, 5 mins]*

A steep paved street almost opposite leads up into the centre of the village, and a short distance along the road to the right there is a roadside taverna.

To complete the circular walk back to Skala Sikamineas there are two options:-

a. Turn right along the road until you reach a path leading down to the right shortly before the taverna. There is a map here of local

footpaths (unhelpful unless you already know the area) and a fingerpost to ΛΕΠΕΤΥΜΝΟΣ. *[a1. 21.68'/17.64']*

(**NB** The following distances and timings restart from this point: the path has been waymarked with red squares fixed to trees).

Follow the path down - the first few metres are paved and very steep - for ten minutes until it crosses a stream and begins to climb again. It runs below and more or less parallel with the road until a junction with a path coming in downhill from the left.
[a2. 21.80'/17.44', 480m, 15 mins] (There is another fingerpost here). Continue straight ahead, until the next T-junction.
[a3. 21.85'/17.46', 580m/100m, 3 mins] Turn left, then continue ahead, with walls on both sides of the path.

A stretch of kalderimi climbs briefly to a path on the right signposted to ΠΡΟΦΗΤΗΣ ΗΛΙΑΣ ΑΔΙΕΞ ΟΔΟΣ (Profitis Ilias – dead end), then descends on steps. Go down through woodland with a wall on the right, to the bottom of a valley and a stream, and continue on the other side on the level on a soft path, with a view of the sea down on the right. (10 mins)

The path leads back into trees and descends again. It bends round to the right and climbs on kalderimi. Go through a gate and bear left, with the entrance to an olive grove straight ahead. Climb steeply over a brow and down again with a wall on the right. In five minutes, continue ahead through a gate on a path along a terrace wall. *[a4. 21.94'/17.00', 1.40km/820m, 30 mins]* (There is a waymark here - if the gate is closed take no notice of the apparent alternative path leading up to the left into an olive grove). At the end of the terrace bear right and continue along the path with steep terracing down on the right towards the sea.

In another five minutes, by an entrance on the left over a fallen wall into an olive grove, go straight ahead along an overgrown kalderimi running between walls. Bear right and continue slightly uphill. Go along the path as it reverts to kalderimi leading down and across a stream *[a5. 22.03'/16.69', 1.90km/500m, 10 mins]*, then bending right under a high stone wall on the other side. It finally bends left and climbs twenty metres to join a concrete road by a yellow trekking trail sign. *[a6. 22.08'/16.66', 2.00km/100m, 5 mins]* Turn right on to the road and follow it downhill.

The two routes merge again here. The description continues at the end of route b.

b Alternatively, for a slightly longer route taking in the ruins of Chalikas, which however involves a further 40 minutes of often steep climbing:

(**NB** The following distances and timings restart from this point)

Turn right, and walk along the road through the foot of the village. Pass the taverna, and continue until the road bends sharp right. On the left immediately after the bend, next to a disused olive mill, there is a fingerpost to ΑΓ ΑΝΝΑ and a yellow trekking trail sign. *[b1. 21.53'/17.45', 636m, 10 mins]*

Take the footpath leading uphill diagonally away from the road (there is an extremely steep and loose path leading directly up hill, which cuts out the first zig-zag, but the extra effort involved is not worth any small time saving). At the first junction, with a chainlink fence on the right, turn sharp left (the path ahead here leads back to the road) and continue uphill. *[b2. 21.57'/17.44', 716m/80m, 4 mins]*

The path varies between kalderimi, loose stone, and earth and continues to climb. It divides for a few metres before coming together again. *[b3. 21.73'/17.28', 1.13km/414m, 10 mins]*

Where the kalderimi goes off to the left uphill opposite a yellow gate *[b4. 21.68'/17.24', 1.23m/100m, 5 mins]*, take the path leading straight ahead (this may be overgrown in places).

The path finally reaches its summit and starts to descend. *[b5. 21.59'/16.97', 1.70km/470m, 10 mins]* After a final steep and rocky descent it emerges on to a track. *[b6. 21.47'/16.64', 2.28km/580m, 17 mins]*

Bear right downhill on the track, across a stream and round to the right (the healing shrine of St Anne – Αγ Άννα - is up an inconspicuous path to the left on this corner). After ten minutes take the path leading off downhill to the right, signposted ΧΑΛΙΚΑΣ. *[b7. 21.66'/16.52', 2.69km/410m, 10 mins]*

Follow it down to a terrace with a drinking fountain in the wall on the left (the Turkish inscription notwithstanding this has been recently installed or reinstated). *[b8. 21.73'/16.51', 2.80km/110m, 5 mins]*

Go down the steps and follow the stony path round the edge of the ruined village. In a few minutes the path bends left to a junction. Take the path ahead through the ruins (the broad kalderimi to the right leads down to the main Vafios - Sikaminia road near the junction to Lepetimnos) and follow it down to the road. *[b9. 21.79'/16.51', 2.99km/190m, 7 mins]*

Turn left on to the road and walk up to a gap in the crash barrier on the opposite side, where there is a finger-post and yellow trekking trail sign. *[b10. 21.79'/16.46', 3.06km/70m, 2 mins]* Go through the gap and follow the path to the right and then downhill to join the road at the edge of Lepetimnos village. Turn left on to the road, then take the first right and follow round left to the village church. *[b11. 21.89'/16.47', 3.25km/190m, 10 mins]*

Take the path to the right of the church gate, which leads down to a concrete road below the village. *[b12. 21.96'/16.59', 3.47km/220m, 5 mins]* Turn right here, and follow the road downhill until you see a finger-post and trekking trail sign at the beginning of an inconspicuous path on the right. *[b13. 22.08'/16.66', 3.73km/260m, 5 mins]*

The two routes merge again here. Total distances from here on are for route **a**, add 1.73km to arrive at route **b** totals.

Continue down the road, which divides after five hundred metres *[14. 22.22'/16.44', 2.50km/500m, 5 mins]* - both branches lead down to the sea; the left-hand one makes for a longer walk (turn left again at the junction near the bottom of the hill), but comes out on the coast road *[15. 22.66'/15.59']* only a few metres from a tiny beach taverna (turn left on to the coast road) which is worth a visit in season for a beer or whatever food is available (often fresh fish

caught by the owner's husband).

If you follow the right-hand branch, and ignore side turnings, you will reach the sea by a small chapel and picnic area owned by the community of Lepetimnos. *[16. 22.63'/16.04', 4.20km/1.70km, 25 mins]*

Turn right on to the unsurfaced coast road and follow it back into Skala Sikaminias *[17. 22.42'/18.18', 7.42km/3.22km, 40 mins]*.

Argenos, Chalikas and Vigla Circular

Total distance 12 kilometres (8.25 km outward, 3.75 km return).

Walking time 4 hours 45 mins
(2 hours 30 mins outward, 2 hours 15 mins return)

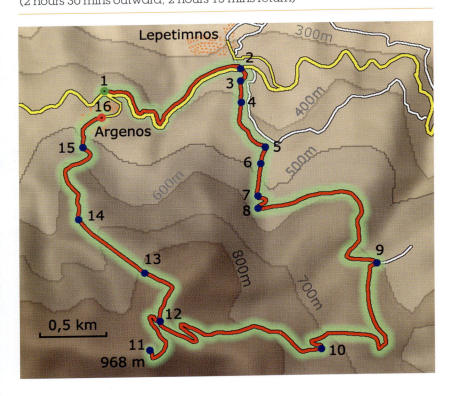

This walk is fairly strenuous in parts with a long and moderately difficult stretch of rocky and precipitous mountainside. It takes in the ruined village of Chalikas and the forested slopes of the Lepetimnos mountain range, before climbing to the highest point in northern Lesvos. There is constant local argument whether Vigla or

Olympos, the imposing white mountain in the south of the island near Agiasos, is the higher - both are officially 968m (3176'). The northerners claim Olympos was lower until the building of the foundations for the television masts on its summit: the opposing view says that the levelling of the summit in preparation for building robbed it of its previous pre-eminence.

The Municipality of Molivos has cleared, signposted and waymarked a series of trails in this area, including most of those used in the lower reaches of this walk. They are mapped on a board in Chalikas, and also in the 'new' village of Lepetimnos and in Sikaminia.

To reach the starting point from Molivos or Petra you need a car or taxi; these instructions assume the former. Take the Vafios road out of Molivos and continue from Vafios as far as Argenos, where you can park on the steep entrance road to the village. (The local bus also parks here when not in use - be sure to leave it plenty of room).

From the main road junction [1. 39°21.70'/26°15.83'], walk downhill to the spring of the Archangel (ΤΑΞΙΑΡΧΗΣ) on the right. (On the left of the road there are the remains of an old water mill once fed by the spring).

Down on the left on a level plateau you will see the village of Lepetimnos, built to accommodate the inhabitants of Chalikas after their village was largely destroyed and abandoned after a landslide over forty years ago. In another two or three minutes the first ruins of Chalikas come into view above the road to the right, and shortly afterwards yellow trekking trail signs and finger-posts on both sides of the road. [2. 21.79'/16.51', 1.35km, 15 mins]

Just before the trekking trail sign on the right, go up a stony path through the ruins of the old village to a junction, where a kalderimi comes in from the left. There is a trail sign-board here. Most of the remaining ruins lie to the right of this junction, but to continue the walk go ahead for a few metres and then follow the rough path round to the right. Continue along the edge of the village and up steps to a T-junction. A restored Turkish fountain has been installed here with an impressive working tap. *[3. 21.73'/16.51', 1.52km/170m, 8 mins]*

Turn left at the top of the steps; go along in front of the fountain on a narrow kalderimi and continue through a gate. After a few metres there is a red trekking trail marker on the left.

The path leads up to join a track. *[4. 21.66'/16.52', 1.65km/130m, 5 mins]* Turn left and follow it until it bends left to cross a stream (there is a sign to Αγ Άννα at this point, a small healing shrine hidden on the hillside to the right) and then right. *[5. 21.47'/16.64', 2.11km/460m, 10 mins]* There should be a fingerpost at this point - follow the track towards KPHTA. (There is a marked footpath off into the woods ahead which leads to Sikaminia - see **Walk 23**).

The track soon doubles back to the right across the stream - go straight ahead along the path signposted to KPITA (the Greek spelling varies from sign to sign). *[6. 21.41'/16.60', 2.25km/140m, 5 mins]* (Where the path leaves the track stay on the left of the stream bed. Since the path was made the course of the stream has

changed with winter torrents and in places you may have to pick your way over boulders. In autumn the path can also be obscured by a deep covering of fallen leaves). Part way along this path the red waymarks end, but carry on among giant ancient plane trees until it rejoins the track. *[7. 21.28'/16.60', 2.50km/250m, 15 mins]*

Turn left uphill, follow round to the right, and arrive at a Turkish fountain (dated 1241AH, ie 1826AD) on the right at the next left-hand bend (this area is KPHTA). This is the last convenient shady spot for a while, and a good place to stop for refreshment. *[8. 21.26'/16.58', 2.66km/160m, 5 mins]*

The track now continues uphill to the left and then levels out to run round the contours of the mountain. Follow it along with Lepetimnos village and the sea visible below on the left. Ignore tracks coming in from the right (barred by iron gates) and left. The track runs gently downhill, then bends left to wind round the head of a deep valley and climb again with Sikaminia and Skala Sikaminias far below on the left, before finally coming to a T-junction with another broad track. *[9. 21.02'/17.19', 4.15km/1.49km, 25 mins]*

Turn right. Almost immediately the track bends sharp left and leads between private fenced and gated groves. Ignore another track forking off downhill to the left, and stay on the main track as it bends up right round the end of a ridge. The television masts on the summit of Mirivilli are now dead ahead, with the summit of Vigla further to the left.

The track continues to wind uphill until a right-hand hairpin encloses two old circular threshing floors and a large water trough.
[10. 20.69'/16.92', 5.54km/1.39km, 25 mins] Ignore another track to the left shortly after this, and go on uphill for another thirty minutes until a concrete road drops away to the right to cross the saddle to Mirivilli. Continue round to the left and climb for another five minutes: the track ends at a fence enclosing the summit of Vigla. Carry on up a rough path to the summit. (The observation cabin here contains radio equipment and is kept locked when unoccupied, though there is nothing to stop you climbing the iron staircase to the door. During the summer months there is a local fireman on watch during daylight hours). *[11. 20.69'/16.03', 8.25km/2.71km, 40 mins]*

To return to Argenos

Come back down from the summit of Vigla and follow the track past the first right-hand hairpin, and then go sharp left.
[12. 20.81'/16.10', 8.81km/560m, 20 mins]

The partly concrete track leads across the saddle to the television masts on the summit of Mirivilli. Before reaching the masts go to the left and look along the line of the power cables which come across the valley to supply the transmitters. The cables run across to a ridge, and then towards the end of a track near another, smaller mast. In turn that track runs down behind the far hill to the village of Argenos, which is visible below to the right.

Higher up the valley to the left of the power-lines you will see a small path running roughly parallel to them. From the transmitters follow down to the first electricity pole, and then follow the path across to the far ridge. Especially at the beginning it is steep and on loose scree: take it slowly and carefully and be sure of your footing.

Once you reach the ridge *[13. 20.99'/16.03', 9.46km/650m, 50 mins]*, cross it and continue along near the top; although still rocky and steep in places, the going is now mostly firm and easier. Ahead on the right of the ridge you will see the end of a track - this is your target.

(After about fifteen minutes (350m) a track comes into view down to the left. If you wish you can go diagonally down to join it, but below the ridge the hillside is very steep and covered in loose scree - it is difficult and hazardous going and hardly worth the effort. Should you do so, however, go right on reaching the track and walk along to a junction by two small radio masts to rejoin the described route).

When you reach the beginning of the track *[14. 21.21'/15.71', 10.11km/650m, 30 mins]*, follow it downhill past a junction by two small radio masts and continue down until it reaches Argenos sports ground (ΑΘΛΗΤΙΚΟ ΣΤΑΔΙΟ ΑΡΓΕΝΟΥ) and a small cemetery. Here the track becomes a concrete road and forks. *[15. 21.49'/15.73', 11.81km/1.70km, 30 mins]*

Take the right fork and follow the road into the village. At the T-junction at the end, turn left and immediately right, then right again in a small square in front of a marble fountain. Turn right once more to reach the village square and cafenions. *[16. 21.60'/15.84', 12.00km/190m, 5 mins]*

Follow the road running downhill from here for a few metres to return to your car.

A Circular walk from Agia Paraskevi to Klopedi, Taxiarchis Monastery, and Kremasti Bridge

25

Total distance 11.5 kilometres

 Walking time 3 hours 30 mins

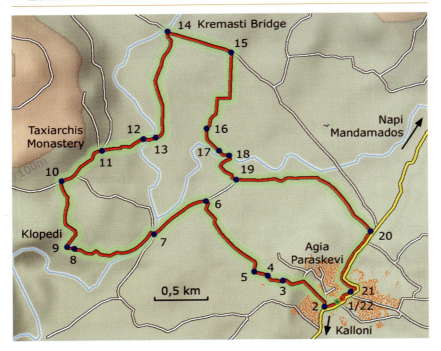

This walk, based on one devised and mapped by the Municipality of Agia Paraskevi, takes in the main sites of historical interest in the area. It leads through a pastoral landscape of meadows, oak woodland, and rivers (which at the right times of year may even have water flowing in them), completely different from the more rugged terrain a few kilometres to the north on the other side of the Lepetimnos range.

The walk starts and finishes in Agia Paraskevi, an attractive town with some impressive public buildings, notably the neo-classical school, built in 1923 (ΕΚΠΑΙΔΕΥΤΗΡΙΑ ΑΓΙΑΣ ΠΑΡΑΣΚΕΥΗΣ), and town hall (ΔΗΜΑΡΧΕΙΟ). It is comparatively untouched by tourism, its prosperity coming from the fertile agricultural land in its administrative area. Its main claim to fame is the annual festival of the bull in late May or early June, but it is also home to the Museum of Industrial Olive Oil Production in Lesvos (on the left as you enter the town from Kalloni), and the Lesbian Wild Life Hospital. The latter, run on a shoe-string by a Dutch couple, is reliant on voluntary donations and welcomes visitors (phone in advance 22530 32006).

If you are driving to Agia Paraskevi come from the direction of Kalloni and park in the large public car park directly behind the school, on your right as you approach the town centre. From the car park, walk back to the main street. The walk starts and finishes on the corner by the war memorial [1. 39°14.81′/26°16.27′].

From the start walk back towards Kalloni (ie with the school on your left), as far as the first junction opposite the town hall (ΔΗΜΑΡΧΕΙΟ). *[2. 14.79′/16.18′, 200m, 2 mins]* Turn right – in a few metres there is an information board on the right with a map and some details of the route on which this walk is based. Continue along this street, and follow the finger-post signs to Klopedi at the next four junctions:- at the first go straight ahead, fork right at the second, and left at the third and fourth. At the fourth junction, in addition to a finger-post, there is metal sign to 'Σπήλαιο Αγ Παρασκευής – Temple of Ag Paraskevi' (Σπήλαιο actually means cave).

At the first unmarked junction immediately after this, keep left up a steep concrete road. This levels out on to a track, which bears to the right, with the hill of Profitis Ilias on the right, and striking weathered rock formations across the field to the left.

The track passes another information board *[3. 14.95'/15.90', 900m/700m, 15 mins]*, and comes to an end at the top of a small field, with farm buildings ahead and to the right. Go down the field towards the buildings ahead and through the gate to their right. *[4. 14.95'/15.81', 1.07km/170m, 5 mins]* Go straight ahead across the field, and then bend right around the end of a mound (there is a small solitary tree with a red waymark on the mound) towards a gate (with another waymark). *[5. 15.00'/15.71', 1.25km/180m, 5 mins]*   Go through the gate on to a path leading ahead. It bends left and leads downhill to come out on to a track. *[6. 15.32'/15.42', 2.13km/880m, 20 mins]* (These paths can also at times become streams).

Turn left, past a fingerpost a few metres along on the right, ignore a side track to the right shortly afterwards, and continue past a farm on the left to a T-junction. *[7. 15.16'/15.09', 2.70km/570m, 10 mins]*   Turn right (signposted ΚΛΟΠΕΔΗ) across the river on Prini's Bridge and then left along the opposite bank. The track bends away from the river and starts to climb, until it comes to an end at a chapel (Taxiarchis) with a large water cistern behind it. *[8. 15.08'/14.56', 3.60km/900m, 10 mins]*

From here a small path climbs a few metres away to the right to the entrance of the Klopedi temple. *[9. 15.10'/14.52', 3.66km/60m, 2 mins]* Unfortunately the site seems to be permanently closed. Go round to the left of the building on to a track (it will probably be necessary to climb a fence) and go uphill to the right. At the first left-hand bend there is an information board on the left; opposite it, over the fence on the right, are the remains of the temple, as well as views across to the Gulf of Kalloni. The temple may have been dedicated to the Apollo of Napi by the citizens of Arisvi, and dates from the 8th to 6th centuries BC.

Carry on along this track until a T-junction *[10. 15.43′/14.49′, 4.41km/750m, 18 mins]*, then turn right on to a dirt road, keeping left where it forks, until you come to the Taxiarchis Monastery on the roadside to your right. (The grounds and chapel are usually open to visitors). *[11. 15.59′/14.75′, 4.90km/490m, 7 mins]* Founded in the 16th century, it is a satellite (Μετοχἰ) of the monastery at Leimonos, and is dedicated to the archangels (Ταξιάρχης) Michael and Gabriel.

Take the concrete track running down alongside the monastery, and follow it to the river. *[12. 15.65′/15.00′, 5.23km/330m, 10 mins]* The path resumes about 300 metres upstream on the other side of the river. *[13. 15.66′/15.09′, 5.52km/290m, 10 mins]* Cross at the most convenient point.

(**Warning**:- Early and late in the year you may have to wade – the bottom is rocky and slippery: do not attempt to cross if the water is too high or fast; return to the monastery and take the track to the right as far as the dirt road to Kremasti, then turn right, follow it to Kremasti bridge, and resume the route from there).

Follow the path up to a junction, bear left, and continue along the dirt and concrete road until it finishes opposite the ancient pack-horse bridge at Kremasti. *[14. 16.21'/15.19', 6.69km/1.17km, 14 mins]* Built in the 14th or 15th century, this was once part of an important trade route between Mitilini and the north of the island, and its slim single arch has survived six hundred years in almost perfect condition.

From the bridge follow the dirt road uphill to the right, and continue as it changes to concrete and runs downhill. Shortly before the end of the concrete turn right into a lane. *[15. 16.11'/15.58', 7.30km/610m, 8 mins]*

This too is concrete at first, and runs straight ahead through farmland with the hill of Profitis Ilias in the distance ahead. It finally bends right to a T-junction at a farm. Turn left here, and continue past another farm to a three-way junction by large farm buildings. *[16. 15.70'/15.41', 8.21km/910m, 15 mins]*

Take the left-hand track (signposted to Agia Paraskevi). It bends left across a stream and up to a farm. Here the track ends and becomes a kalderimi footpath. Turn right at the next T-junction and follow the path to a river. *[17. 15.58'/15.49', 8.57km/360m, 7 mins]*

Go to the left along the river bank (don't be tempted by the apparent continuation of the path directly opposite – it leads nowhere) to a finger-post then cross to a path to the left of more farm buildings *[18. 15.56'/15.55', 8.68km/110m, 5 mins]*, go up it and continue on a narrow track. At the next T-junction turn left. *[19. 15.44'/15.63', 9.04km/360m, 6 mins]*

Walk along this track, with views to the left across the fertile valley to the Lepetimnos mountain range, until you come to a T-junction with an asphalt road. (This is the road from Agia Paraskevi to the village of Napi, leading on to Mandamados). *[20. 15.17'/16.48', 10.52km/1.48km, 20 mins]*

Turn right on to the road. After a few metres there is a sign pointing ahead to 'Agia Paraskevi Center'. Keep on the asphalt road as you enter the town. It bends left, then right, and becomes stone paved as it approaches the centre, a cross-roads with a large cafenion facing you. *[21. 14.85'/16.34', 11.26km/740m, 15 mins]* Go half-right ahead, to the right of the cafenion, and in two minutes you are back at your starting point. *[22. 14.81'/16.27', 11.35km/90m, 2 mins]*